Language Essentials for Teachers of

for
Early Childhood
Educators

Lucy Hart Paulson, Ed.D., CCC-SLP
Louisa C. Moats, Ed.D.

and
Contributing Author J. Ron Nelson, Ph.D.

BOSTON, MA | LONGMONT, CO

Copyright 2010 Cambium Learning Sopris West®.
All rights reserved.

10 B&B   16 15

ISBN-13: 978-1-60218-502-9
ISBN-10: 1-60218-502-6
JDE#: 165956/312/05-15

No portion of this work may be reproduced or transmitted in any form
or by any means, electronic or mechanical, including photocopying or recording,
or by any information storage and retrieval system, without the express written
permission of the publisher.

Printed in the United States of America
Published and Distributed by

Cambium
LEARNING®
Sopris West®

4093 Specialty Place • Longmont, Colorado 80504
(303) 651-2829 • www.soprislearning.com

How does copyright pertain to LETRS® *for Early Childhood Educators?*

- It is illegal to reproduce any part of the LETRS *for Early Childhood Educators* book in any way and for any reason without written permission from the copyright holder, Cambium Learning Sopris West®. This applies to copying, scanning, retyping, etc.
- It is illegal to reproduce LETRS *for Early Childhood Educators* materials to distribute or present at a workshop without written permission from the copyright holder.
- It is illegal to use the name LETRS in association with any workshop, materials, training, publications, etc., without written permission from the copyright holder.

Acknowledgments

Throughout my career, I have had the good fortune of getting to know many young children with diverse abilities and watch them grow and develop. I have seen them learn to talk and followed them as they learned to read, observing the powerful connection between oral language and literacy development.

Through the years, I have had the privilege of working with many gifted early childhood educators. I am thankful for all I have learned from them and for their commitment to the young children in their care. I also am grateful for their participation in guiding our understanding of what young children do, what they need, and how we can help them develop to their fullest potential.

I would like to express my deep appreciation for all the support and understanding provided by my family, particularly Mitch, who always picks up and carries on for me, and Lynnea, who is so steadfast. Lara, who was born an artist, has been enriching my life with images. Her drawings are treasures. Thanks to my colleagues for their assistance, ideas, edits, and encouragement throughout the process, particularly Rebecca Johns, a true believer.

Louisa Moats and Steve Mitchell have been the guiding forces behind this module, bringing a comprehensive understanding of the importance of the early years in building a strong foundation for learning to read and write. Thank you for your commitment to our youngest learners, their teachers, and for the opportunity to participate in this project. Finally, thank you to Holly Bell and the editorial and production staffs at Sopris West for their help, guidance, and support throughout this whole process.

—LHP

About the Authors

Lucy Hart Paulson, Ed.D., CCC-SLP, is a speech-language pathologist by profession and holds a doctorate degree in education with a focus in early literacy. She has many years of experience working with young children and their families in public school, Head Start, private, and university settings. Dr. Paulson is a faculty member in the Communicative Sciences and Disorders program and the director of the Western Montana RiteCare Language and Literacy Clinic at The University of Montana.

She brings a unique and broad-based perspective to early childhood development, blending together areas of social communication, language, and literacy, which result in effective and engaging interventions for children of all ages and abilities. Dr. Paulson is the lead author of *Building Early Literacy and Language Skills* (BELLS; Paulson, Noble, Jepson, & van den Pol, 2001) and *Good Talking Words* (Paulson & van den Pol, 1998), a social communication skills program for young children.

Louisa Moats, Ed.D., is well known for her publications on reading instruction, the professional development of teachers, and the relationship between language, reading, and spelling. She has published in many peer-reviewed journals and written numerous books and book chapters. Dr. Moats authored the American Federation of Teachers' "Teaching Reading **Is** Rocket Science," Learning First Alliance's "Every Child Reading: A Professional Development Guide," and The Reading First Leadership Academy's "Blueprint for Professional Development." Her professional development program, *Language Essentials for Teachers of Reading and Spelling* (LETRS®), evolved from Dr. Moats' many years of experience teaching classroom teachers and reading specialists in graduate programs and in school systems.

Dr. Moats began her career as a teacher of students with learning problems. After earning a doctorate in reading from Harvard University, she became a licensed psychologist for 15 years. Dr. Moats then assumed responsibility for a major five-year National Institutes of Health (NIH)-funded research project in Washington, D.C., during which she learned the importance of modeling instruction for teachers in training.

J. Ron Nelson, Ph.D., contributed to the Chapter 5 assessment content as well as appendix material.

Contents

Introduction to LETRS® for Early Childhood Educators . . . 1
    Pre-K Can Work, With Research-Based Practices 1
    The Function of LETRS® *for Early Childhood Educators*. 2

Chapter 1 Early Literacy Connections
    Learner Objectives for Chapter 1 5
    Warm-Up 5
The Foundations of Early Literacy 6
    Exercise 1.1: Environmental Supports. 6
    Table 1.1: Essential Components of Early Literacy Development. 7
    Figure 1.1: Early Literacy Building Blocks and Associated Component Skills. 8
    Exercise 1.2: Foundations for the Essential Components. 8
Phonological Processing 9
    Figure 1.2: The Three Components of Phonological Processing 10
    Exercise 1.3: How the Phonological Processing System Works. 11
    Exercise 1.4: A Young Child's Phonological Production 13
Phonological Processing in Reading 13
    Figure 1.3: The Four-Part Processing Model for Word Recognition 14
    Exercise 1.5: Phonological Processor vs. Orthographic Processor 14
Developmentally Appropriate Practice in Early Literacy 15
    Exercise 1.6: Rate Your Current Beliefs. 16
Wrap-Up 17
Reflection and Review. 18

Chapter 2 The Oral Language Connection to Literacy
    Learner Objectives for Chapter 2 19
    Warm-Up 19
Structures of Oral Language 20
    Table 2.1: Rule-Ordered Systems of Languages. 21
    Phonology. 21
        Figure 2.1: English Vowel Phonemes by Order of Articulation 22
        Exercise 2.1: Singing With Vowels and Consonants 23
        Consonant Characteristics: Place, Manner, and Voicing 23
        Exercise 2.2: Evaluate Consonant Sounds 23
        Exercise 2.3: Select a Sound for Instruction 24
        Table 2.2: Voiced and Voiceless Consonant Cognates 25
        Exercise 2.4: Consonant Sounds With Voicing 25
        Exercise 2.5: Phonemic Awareness: Count the Phonemes 26
        Spanish Phonology. 26
        AAE Phonological Patterns. 27
    Semantics 27
        Table 2.3: Expressive Vocabulary Timeline of Young Children 27

Contents

    Exercise 2.6: List Vocabulary Words in a Storybook 28
  Morphology 28
    Exercise 2.7: Add Morphological Endings 29
    Exercise 2.8: Divide Words by Syllables and Morphemes 30
    Table 2.4: Summary of Six Types of Syllables in Written English 31
    Exercise 2.9: Locate Morphemes 31
  Syntax 32
    Exercise 2.10: Quantify Sentence Length 32
  Prosody 33
    Exercise 2.11: Experiment With Prosodic Stress 33
Typical Developmental Stages of Oral and Written Language 34
  Stage 1 (Oral: Prelexic) (Written: Prelogographic) 34
  Stage 2 (Oral: Lexic) (Written: Logographic, or Prealphabetic) 35
  Stage 3 (Oral: Systematic Simplification) (Written: Early Alphabetic) 36
  Stage 4 (Oral: Assembly) (Written: Later Alphabetic) 37
  Stage 5 (Oral: Metaphonological) (Written: Consolidated Alphabetic) 38
    Figure 2.2: The Five Developmental Stages of Oral and Written Language 38
    Exercise 2.12: A Case Study 39
    Traits and Implications of Developmental Difficulties 39
Strategies That Facilitate Oral Language Development 40
  Language-Stimulation Techniques 41
    Exercise 2.13: Expand Utterances 41
    Table 2.5: Three Types of Responses in Adult-Child Conversations 42
    Exercise 2.14: Match the Type of Response to the Sentence 42
    Exercise 2.15: Practice Language Modeling 43
    Scaffolding Strategies 44
    Table 2.6: Read-Aloud Scaffolding Techniques 44
    Exercise 2.16: Practice Scaffolding 45
    Questioning Strategies 45
    Figure 2.3: Question Hierarchy 46
    Exercise 2.17: Identify the Hierarchy of Questions 46
    Dialogic Storybook Reading 46
  Wrap-Up 47
  Reflection and Review 48

Chapter 3 Phonological Awareness Connections

  Learner Objectives for Chapter 3 51
  Warm-Up 51
What Is Phonological Awareness? 52
    Exercise 3.1: Phonological or Phonemic Awareness? 52
  Component Skills of Phonological Awareness 52
  How Phonological Awareness Develops 54
    Rhyming 54
    Table 3.1: Age at Which Rhyming Skills Begin to Develop 54
    Exercise 3.2: List Rhyming Words 55
    Exercise 3.3: Generate Rhyming Words 56
    Alliteration 58
    Table 3.2: Age at Which Alliteration Skills Begin to Develop 58

  Exercise 3.4: Isolate Initial Sounds 58
  Blending. 59
   Table 3.3: Age at Which Blending Skills Begin to Develop 60
   Exercise 3.5: Determine the Level of Linguistic Analysis. 60
  Segmenting 60
   Table 3.4: Age at Which Segmenting Skills Begin to Develop. 61
   Exercise 3.6: Identify Syllables and Phonemes 61
   Figure 3.1: Picture Puzzle Formats for Blending and Segmenting 64
 Hierarchy of Phonological Awareness Skill Development. 64
  Table 3.5: Phonological Awareness Skills in Developmental Order. 65
  Table 3.6: Ranking of Percent Correct Scores of Phonological Awareness Skills
  for 4- and 5-year-Old Children 66
 Wrap-Up 66
 Reflection and Review. 67

Chapter 4 Written Language Connections

 Learner Objectives for Chapter 4 69
 Warm-Up 69
Concepts of Print 70
 How Children Develop Print Awareness 71
  Babies and Toddlers. 72
  3- to 4-Year-Olds 72
  4- to 5-Year-Olds 72
 Ways to Help Young Children Develop Print Awareness 72
  Print Awareness for Babies 73
  Print Awareness for Toddlers 73
  Print Awareness for 3- to 4-Year-Olds. 73
  Print Awareness for 4- to 5-Year-Olds. 73
  Exercise 4.1: Inform Instruction About Print Concepts 74
Alphabet Knowledge That Leads to the Alphabetic Principle 75
 Figure 4.1: Foundations of the Alphabetic Principle 75
 How Young Children Synthesize Letters and Words 75
  Table 4.1: The Learning Sequence of Letters and Words 76
 Ways to Help Young Children Learn Their ABCs (and DEFs) 76
  Figure 4.2: ABC/abc Eye Chart. 77
  Exercise 4.2: Make Letter Forms 79
Becoming a Writer: From Scribbles to Letters 79
 Why Writing is Important 79
 The Five Stages of Writing Development 81
  Table 4.2: Typical Writing Development Progression in Young Children 82
  Exercise 4.3: Identify the Levels of Writing Development 83
 Ways to Help Young Children Understand the Importance of Print 85
  "Picture Story/Word Story" Strategy 85
  Exercise 4.4: Write at Different Levels of Print 88
  Sharing Ideas. 88
  Exercise 4.5: Modeling Writing. 89
 Wrap-Up 89
 Reflection and Review. 89

Contents

Chapter 5 Assessment Connections

Learner Objectives for Chapter 5 91
Warm-Up 91
What Is Assessment? 92
    Exercise 5.1: What Assessments Do You Use? 92
    Table 5.1: Purposes of Preschool Assessment 93
Characteristics of Good Assessments 93
Why Assessment Is Important 94
    Professional Accountability 94
    Early Identification of Difficulties 94
    Predictors of Later Literacy Difficulties 95
    Table 5.2: Early Language Indicators for Later Literacy Difficulties 95
Assessment Characteristics and Scores 96
    Four Types of Formal Assessments for Young Children 97
        Table 5.3: Types of Formal Assessments and Related Functions 98
        Screening Assessments 98
        Progress-Monitoring Assessments 99
        Diagnostic Assessments 100
        Outcome Assessments 101
        Table 5.4: Examples of Early Literacy Assessments and Their Characteristics 101
    Types of Informal Assessments 101
        Examples of Published Informal Assessment Measures 102
        Exercise 5.2: Categorize Your Assessments 102
        Exercise 5.3: Identify the Type of Assessment 103
        The Early Literacy Checklist 104
        Exercise 5.4: Match the Oral Skill to the Language Structure 106
        Exercise 5.5: Indicate the Progression of Phonological Skills 107
        Exercise 5.6: Match Checklist Items to Your Assessments 108
    Wrap-Up 108
    Reflection and Review 108

Glossary 111

References 117

Resources: LETRS® Supplementary Modules 123

Appendix A: Preschool Curricula 125

Appendix B: Understanding Test Scores 127

Appendix C: Developing Preschool Measures 137

Answer Key 143

Introduction to
LETRS® for Early Childhood Educators

Pre-K Can Work, With Research-Based Practices

Agreement among preschool educators is widespread that all children deserve quality learning experiences that are sensitive to their social and emotional needs and that stimulate language, cognitive, and physical development. Children who come from disadvantaged circumstances, such as those eligible for Head Start or Early Reading First, are especially dependent on preschool opportunities that will help them prepare for academic learning. Within that broad consensus, however, preschool programs have differed widely in their emphasis and structure. To resolve some of the ongoing debates about how to best "do" preschool, several large-scale research and consensus-building projects have occurred in the last few years.

One research group led by Duncan, a member of a National Academies of Science panel including 11 co-authors (Duncan et al., 2007), analyzed and collated results from six longitudinal (long-term) studies of the effect of preschool programs on the later academic achievement of 8- to 14-year-olds. The panel's analysis also evaluated the relative impact of three key elements of school readiness—school-entry academic levels; attention skills; and social-emotional characteristics—on later reading and math achievement. In all six studies, children's levels of early academic skills most strongly predicted later academic outcomes; attention skills were the next most important predictor. Surprisingly, social-emotional behaviors were generally not found to be significant predictors of later academic achievement.

Additional support for the importance of early language and cognitive skills for later reading success comes from the preliminary report of the National Early Literacy Panel (National Institute for Literacy [NIFL], 2007). The panel conducted a meta-analysis of approximately 300 existing studies of the effects of preschool programs, environmental characteristics, and child characteristics on later academic achievement. Overall, there was strong support for the importance of alphabet knowledge, phonological awareness, rapid naming tasks, writing/writing name, and phonological short-term memory tasks as predictors of later reading and writing. Somewhat less consistently related were global language development and concepts of print. There was weak evidence for the importance of visual perceptual skills as a predictor of reading and writing. After looking at the effects of programs, the panel concluded that "explicit attempts to build code-related skills; to share books with young children; to enhance oral language; and to use home, preschool, and kindergarten interventions can all be valuable paths to at least some" of the desired outcomes at the preschool level. Young children's language skills, including vocabulary and complex language, phonological awareness, and letter knowledge are the most important and unique predictors of reading ability.

Introduction

Thus, as the importance of preschool becomes more and more apparent, professional development for early childhood educators must emphasize training in instructional practices that will support children's development of these crucial skills. Landry, Anthony, Swank, Gunnewig, & Monseque-Bailey (2007) conducted a large project involving several hundred classrooms in which professional development for teachers was successful in improving student readiness. Professional development that had a strong impact on student learning, especially students at risk for later academic failure, included direct explanation of important component skills and modeling of instruction based on those concepts. Presentations to teachers also included the basic theories that underlie essential program components and methods of instruction, as well as practice carrying out instruction in playful ways that work with young children. The use of progress-monitoring assessments and follow-up mentoring and coaching in teachers' classrooms were also essential for promoting student gains.

The best instruction for children includes a balance between child-centered and teacher-directed approaches to learning (Landry, Swank, Smith, Assel, & Gunnewig, 2006; National Association for the Education of Young Children [NAEYC], 2009; NIFL, 2007). It is true that 3- to 4-year-olds learn in semi-structured activities that are playfully carried out, and that teachers should be spontaneous and responsive to children's interests. Importantly, teachers should proceed in a planful way and have in mind clear expectations for learning outcomes. They should know the priorities for student progress as identified by screening, progress monitoring, and observation, and be ready to alter their approach if students are not gaining ground.

In one of the few studies that has compared the relative benefits of preschool curricula, Landry et al. (2006) found differences in the effects among various programs. The type of program chosen did moderate the effects of professional development on children's language development. The strongest programs included components to teach oral language and vocabulary, knowledge of letters, and phonological awareness (also found in earlier studies by Dickinson & Smith, 1994; Frede, 1995; Whitehurst, Arnold, Epstein, Angell, Smith et al., 1994). The use of a focused language and literacy curriculum provided significant benefits, especially in receptive and expressive vocabulary skills, for the children of teachers in their first year of training. Children's vocabulary and phonological awareness were two skill areas that appeared to benefit from teachers receiving a second year of training, indicating that successful implementation of the phonological awareness component of an evidence-based curriculum may take longer for teachers in training. Preschool curricula that have been associated with positive results in these studies and other Early Reading First studies are listed in *Appendix A*.

The Function of LETRS® *for Early Childhood Educators*

LETRS, which stands for *Language Essentials for Teachers of Reading and Spelling* (Moats, 2005a–2010b; see *Resources: LETRS® Supplementary Modules* section), is foundational professional development that teaches the meaning of the scientific research base for delivering effective instruction in reading, language, and writing. The 12 core modules are appropriate for educators in grades K–12, and the content is appropriate for workshop delivery or credit-bearing courses.

This LETRS *for Early Childhood Educators* module is intended to enrich and extend professional development for early childhood educators and care providers in helping pre-kindergarten children learn the early literacy and language skills shown in research to be critical for later success. The information and techniques are also important for kindergarten teachers whose young students have not yet learned these vital early literacy skills needed for success in the first few years of school.

The first of this module's three main goals is to focus on the definitions and concepts related to early literacy and language, the processes involved, and the developmental sequences by which these skills develop. The second goal is to expand strategies used to design and implement rich learning activities that are engaging, effective, evidence-based, and developmentally appropriate. Intentionally planning activities that include learning outcomes in each early literacy foundation optimizes children's learning opportunities. Many of the sample activities come from *Building Early Literacy and Language Skills* (BELLS; Paulson et al., 2001). The final goal is to describe and discuss assessment procedures to make the best use of data in teaching our youngest learners. This important process identifies what children know and guides what they need to be taught.

This module is divided into five topic chapters:
- Chapter 1 defines the foundation components of early literacy, including the role that phonological processing plays in both oral and written language and developmentally appropriate practices in reading and writing.
- Chapter 2 describes the structures of language, the developmental stages that build oral and written language skills, and strategies to enhance these skills.
- Chapter 3 describes the components of phonological awareness, a general continuum of development of these skills, and ways to help young children learn them.
- Chapter 4 focuses on print development in the areas of print awareness concepts, alphabet knowledge, and learning to become a writer.
- Chapter 5 describes the assessment process and the components that need to be included in an assessment.

The strands of child development are intertwined and subject to many influences, with strong relationships among language, literacy, and social and emotional development. Often, challenges in children's behavior are results of social misunderstanding or underdeveloped language competence. While the information in this module will enhance the ability of early childhood educators to improve the language and academic skills that impact children's behavior, there are other considerations (e.g., social communication skills, self-regulation, emotional development) that are beyond its scope. Another significant factor influencing

Introduction

literacy development in many settings is the growing number of children who are learning English as another language (English language learners, or ELLs). The information in this module provides a good foundation of understanding that is pertinent to developing the skills of ELLs.

The early childhood years are crucial to academic and life success. When early childhood educators understand the processes involved in early literacy and language development and intentionally plan activities that enhance these skills, they will create high-quality learning environments for the children in their care.

Early Literacy Connections

This chapter discusses: (a) the foundations of early literacy; (b) the contribution that phonological processing plays in learning oral and written language; and (c) developmentally appropriate practice in preparing young children for learning to read, write, and use the language of the classroom.

Learner Objectives for Chapter 1
- Describe the foundations of early literacy.
- Define the component skills of phonological processing.
- Describe the contribution of phonological processing in oral and written language.
- Describe a blend of instructional approaches in early literacy.

Warm-Up
- What are your thoughts about these questions? Jot down a response for each.
    1. What are the three foundation areas of early literacy?
        _____
        _____

    2. Give an example of a literacy activity you have used with children. What early literacy foundation area does this activity develop?
        _____
        _____

    3. What is the difference between *phonological processing*, *phonological awareness*, and *phonemic awareness*?
        _____
        _____

Chapter 1

4. How does phonological processing contribute to language development? To the reading process?

   _____

   _____

5. What is *phonological representation*, and how does it relate to phonological processing?

   _____

   _____

6. What is the focus of the evidence-based reading research perspective? The emergent literacy perspective?

   _____

   _____

   _____

The Foundations of Early Literacy

Literacy development begins very early in a child's life and lays the foundation for learning to read and write. For our purposes, the term *early literacy* describes the developmental period between birth and 6 years. The more children know about language and literacy before they begin formal schooling, the better equipped they are to succeed in reading (Snow, Burns, & Griffin, 1998).

Exercise 1.1 | Environmental Supports

- List all literacy opportunities you can think of that are typically found in a preschool environment.

   _____

   _____

   _____

   _____

   _____

   _____

Early Literacy Connections

Learning to talk is a natural process, but learning to read is not. While our brains are "wired" to learn the language we are exposed to when we are very young, literacy must be directly taught to most children over several years of formal education. Children need many interactions with adults who talk to them, read and tell stories to them, point out print in their environment, and encourage them to scribble and write messages.

Decades of research underscore the importance of the early childhood years for building foundational literacy development (Neuman & Dickinson, 2002; Snow et al., 1998). Spoken and written language have a reciprocal relationship, interacting to bolster language and literacy competence. Children with spoken language problems frequently have difficulty learning to read and write, and children with reading and writing problems frequently have difficulty with spoken language. Children who get off to a poor start in reading rarely catch up. Early intervention is considerably more efficient and effective than taking a "wait and see" approach. It takes four times as long to remediate a student's poor reading skills in fourth grade as in kindergarten or early first grade (Lyon & Fletcher, 2001).

Foundations of early literacy are formed as children: (1) develop competency in oral language; (2) gain an awareness of the sound structure of language (i.e., phonological awareness); and (3) find meaning in the written symbols they see around them, including an understanding of being a writer (Blachman, 1991; Snow et al., 1998; van Kleeck, 1998; Whitehurst & Lonigan, 1998). These three major areas (see *Table 1.1*) have been identified by research as the essential components of early literacy development, and each will be explored in greater depth in this module.

Table 1.1 Essential Components of Early Literacy Development

Oral Language	Phonological Awareness	Print Knowledge
(speaking and listening)	(the conscious awareness of and the ability to manipulate the sound structures of spoken language)	(print awareness concepts, alphabet knowledge, and being a writer)

Oral language. By the time children reach their first birthday, they already know a lot about speaking and listening *if they have been spoken to frequently*. They recognize speech sounds and know which sounds are in the words that are important to them. As they grow older, they learn new words at an incredible rate, and they learn how to use those words in conversation to express their needs, wants, and ideas.

Phonological awareness. Considered essential for reading an alphabetic language, phonological awareness is an ability to "play" with words and involves two parts: the sensitivity to the sound structures of language, and the ability to reflect on spoken words to consciously manipulate the syllables and speech sounds (i.e., phonemes) in words.

Print knowledge. Knowing that spoken words are represented by written symbols is a first step in learning to read. Print knowledge includes three component areas: concepts of print, alphabet knowledge, and being a writer.

Figure 1.1 illustrates that competency in the three early literacy building blocks provides the foundation for learning the component skills of literacy: phonemic awareness, phonics, vocabulary, fluency, and comprehension (National Reading Panel [NRP], 2000), along with writing and spelling (Moats, 2005/2006).

Figure 1.1 Early Literacy Building Blocks and Associated Component Skills

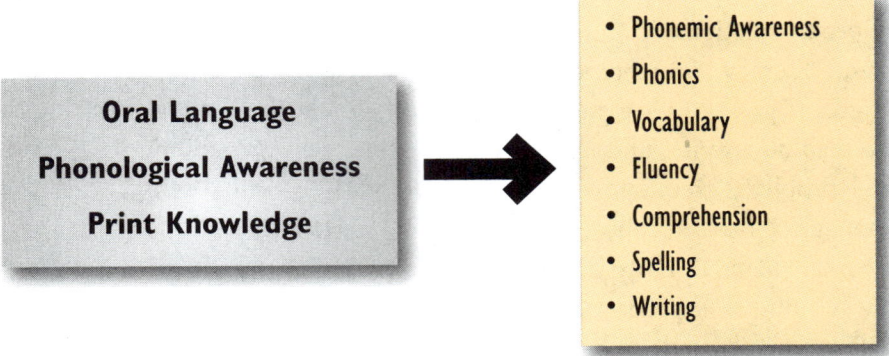

Exercise 1.2 — Foundations for the Essential Components

- What early literacy foundation area is necessary for each reading and writing component?

Early Literacy Area	Reading/Writing Component
_____	Phonemic awareness
_____	Phonics
_____	Vocabulary
_____	Fluency
_____	Comprehension
_____	Spelling
_____	Writing

Oral language directly relates to vocabulary and comprehension, and peripherally relates to all other literacy components. Phonological awareness is the foundation for phonemic awareness, phonics, and spelling. Print knowledge contributes to phonics, fluency, and writing. However, each early literacy foundation is needed for each component of literacy. As early childhood educators, our job is to:
- know what the desired early literacy learning outcomes are;
- provide learning opportunities and activities based on children's learning needs; and
- evaluate children's learning **and** the effectiveness of the activities.

Phonological Processing

An underlying foundation of both oral and written language is phonological processing. In order to learn to talk, a child needs to process the sounds of language. The same is true when children learn to read and write.

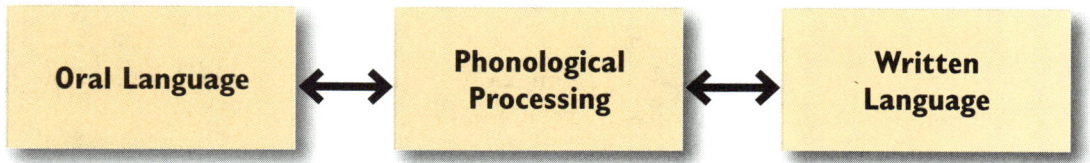

Phonological processing is the ability to understand and use the sound system of a language to process oral and written information. It entails multiple functions: perceiving, interpreting, storing (remembering), recalling/retrieving, and generating the sounds of language (Moats, 2009).

The development of phonological processing begins before birth. Newborns are able to identify their mothers' voices by the way they *sound*. Babies listen to the sounds of the language they are exposed to and are able to distinguish between the speech sounds that are part of their language from speech sounds spoken in other languages (Gopnik, Meltzoff, & Kuhl, 1999). As babies coo and babble, they are practicing, producing, and listening to the speech sounds of the language they hear. This time of life is vital in the development of phonological processing.

As young children develop an expressive vocabulary, they learn to say the words they have heard within their environment, using the speech sounds that are part of the word structures. The definition of a *word* in an expressive form includes two components: a *consistent phonological form* that is similar to the adult form and a *consistent referent* (McLaughlin, 1998). A baby saying "ba" (a consistent phonological form) while holding a ball (a consistent referent) is using a word. As children's vocabularies grow, they are able to remember words more accurately and to differentiate between words with similar-sounding structures. In part, this is a result of their developing phonological processing skills.

Chapter 1

> **Phonological processing is a part of word-learning at several levels:**
> - "Hearing" or being aware of the sounds of words
> - Saying words
> - Remembering words accurately
> - Differentiating words that sound similar (Moats, 2003)

Research has identified three components of phonological processing abilities (*Figure 1.2*): phonological awareness, phonological memory, and phonological naming along with the related skill of phonological representation. These components are strongly related to subsequent reading acquisition (Anthony & Francis, 2005; Lonigan, 2006; Wagner, Torgesen, & Rashotte, 1994; Whitehurst & Lonigan, 2002).

Figure 1.2 The Three Components of Phonological Processing

PHONOLOGICAL PROCESSING
- Phonological Awareness
- Phonological Memory
- Phonological Naming
  - Phonological Representation

Phonological awareness, as previously described, is the ability to *attend to* and *manipulate* the syllables and sounds of words. This component of phonological processing is the most strongly related to literacy (Anthony & Francis, 2005; Lonigan, 2006).

Phonological awareness encompasses a variety of skills, ranging from basic to complex. *Phonemic awareness*, a more sophisticated component of phonological awareness, is the ability to reflect on and consciously manipulate the phonemes or speech sounds in words. An example of an easier phonological awareness skill is clapping syllables in a word, and a more complex phonemic awareness skill is deleting a sound from a given word, such as saying the word **stop** without the /s/ sound.

> **Note**: Speech sounds are represented between two / / marks (e.g., the sound /m/ is represented by the letter **m**).

Early Literacy Connections

Phonological memory is the ability to immediately process and recall sound-based information (i.e., something you have heard) in short-term memory for temporary storage (Anthony & Francis, 2005; Whitehurst & Lonigan, 2002). Think of a time when you were introduced to someone. Even though you heard the person's name, often you cannot remember it. In order to be able to repeat the name, you need to rehearse it or associate it with something else so that you develop a stronger representation of the name in your long-term memory.

Phonological naming is the ability to efficiently retrieve phonological information that is stored in your long-term memory (Lonigan, 2006; Whitehurst & Lonigan, 2002) or, more simply, to quickly think of the word you want to say. For example, think of the name of a close family member (hopefully, that person's name is quickly retrieved because it is prevalent in your long-term memory). Now, think of a time when you ran into someone you had not seen in a long time, and the person's name did not come to you immediately. As you were trying to recall the name, if you were able to retrieve some form of the name such as the beginning sound or the syllable structure, you were probably more likely to retrieve the name. The phonological form helped stimulate the retrieval of the name.

Exercise 1.3 — How the Phonological Processing System Works

- The interrelated components of phonological processing help us manipulate the structures of words. Here is an example of how your phonological processing system works:

    — Say aloud the word for the largest member of the feline family that has orange and black stripes.

    — Then, say the word without the /g/ sound.

    — You said **tiger**, and then fairly easily deducted the word **tire**.

- What phonological processing skills were required for you to complete this task?

    _____

    _____

An important aspect of phonological processing is **phonological representation**, which is the quality or distinctness of words stored in our memory and the ability to access the word representations in a conscious manner (Gillon, 2004). When we learn a new word, we develop a phonological representation of that word or a sense of "inner speech" and what that word sounds like. We also develop distinctions among words with similar phonological properties (i.e., words that sound alike).

Think about that family member's name. Can you "hear" the name even though you have not said it aloud? This is your phonological representation. Here is another example:

As a family was preparing for an outing, the youngest child said, "Doe in da tar." The mother quietly questioned "The tar?" The child admonished, "Not *tar*, **tar**!" This child has not yet developed a distinction between the words **tar** and **car** or a separate phonological representation in his inner speech for each word within his own expressive use of these words.

Phonological representation is important not only for oral vocabulary development but also for written language development. According to Gillon (2004), if children have distinct phonological representations of spoken words, they may be able to more easily access the phonological segments needed for phonological awareness. Children need to have phonological representations of spoken words and learn that words are segmentable (e.g., saying "**di – no – saur**") before they can be expected to identify or manipulate individual phonemes or speech sounds of words in a conscious manner.

An interplay exists between the phonological processes and the representations of spoken words. This interplay changes over time, from whole words to more specific word parts and vocabulary growth (Metsala & Walley, 1998). Young children first learn to recognize and say words as wholly single entities. They then learn to identify words by their underlying phonological structures, such as syllables and sound units. This restructuring of phonological representations of whole words to word parts or segmental units is necessary for the development of explicit phoneme awareness (Rvachew, Nowak, & Cloutier, 2004).

Exercise 1.4 — A Young Child's Phonological Production

- A 4-year-old boy was playing a guessing game to identify a small object. His teacher, who was hiding a toy animal in her hand, asked him, "Guess what I have? **hip – po – po – ta – mus**." The child responded first with "Hippo," and then, because he was aware that the teacher's word was longer than his, said, "Hippopomotamus!"

1. What was this child's phonological representation for this animal?

   _____

   _____

2. Describe how this child used each of these elements of phonological processing:

   Phonological memory _____

   _____

   Phonological awareness _____

   _____

   Phonological naming _____

   _____

Phonological Processing in Reading

Phonological processing is not only crucial to oral language development, it is also an underlying skill in the reading process. Adams (1990) conceptualized a four-part neurological processing system that helps us understand what occurs within our brains as we read (see *Figure 1.3*, next page). The four processors include the orthographic processor, the phonological processor, the meaning processor, and the context processor.

Chapter 1

Figure 1.3 The Four-Part Processing Model for Word Recognition

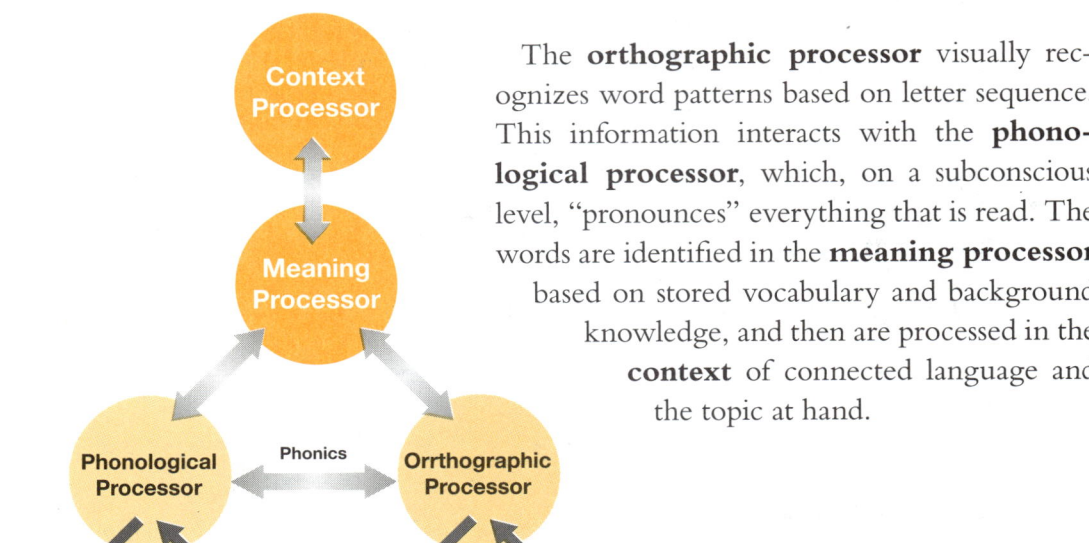

The **orthographic processor** visually recognizes word patterns based on letter sequence. This information interacts with the **phonological processor**, which, on a subconscious level, "pronounces" everything that is read. The words are identified in the **meaning processor** based on stored vocabulary and background knowledge, and then are processed in the **context** of connected language and the topic at hand.

Exercise 1.5 Phonological Processor vs. Orthographic Processor

- Here is a great example of how our phonological processing system works when we are reading. Read this story silently.

LADLE RAT ROTTEN HUT
(Adams, 1990)

Wants pawn term, dare worsted ladle gull hoe lift wetter murder inner ladle cordage honor itch offer lodge dock florist. Disc ladle gull orphan worry ladle cluck wetter putty ladle rat hut, end fur disc raisin pimple colder ladle rat rotten hut. Wan moaning rat rotten hut's murder colder inset: "Ladle rat rotten hut, heresy basking winsome burden barter and shirker cockles. Tick disc ladle basking tudor cordage offer groin murder hoe lifts honor udder site offer florist. Shaker lake, dun stopper laundry wrote, end yonder nor sorghum stenches dun stopper torque wet strainers."

- What is this story about?

  _____

  _____

- How far did you have to read before you knew what the story was about?

  _____

Initially, you may have found it a bit difficult to make sense of the story when looking at the written form. Your *orthographic processor* visually recognized the words, your *meaning processor* identified what the words meant, and your *context processor* was trying to connect a story about a spoon (**ladle**), a rodent (**rat**), something spoiled (**rotten**), and a place to live (**hut**).

These elements do not seem to make sense in relationship to each other. It was not until your *phonological processor* "kicked" in at a higher level, either on its own or when you heard the story read aloud (which automatically increased your level of processing from a phonological basis), that the meaning became clear and you were able to "hear" *ladle rat rotten hut* as *Little Red Riding Hood*.

The neurological research looking at brain functioning has given us a better and deeper understanding of the contribution that the phonological processor makes in the reading process. The quality of the underlying phonological representation, long-term memory for words, and the ability to access this representation using phonological information in a conscious manner is critical for reading and spelling development (Gillon, 2004).

In the past, there was a widely held perception that reading difficulties were based in the visual processing system and were attributable to "seeing" things backwards. However, the neurological science technology available to us today has clearly documented underdeveloped phonological processing in brain activity when reading is a struggle. According to Shaywitz (2003), the vast majority—88 percent—of the dyslexic population, defined as those who experience an unexpected difficulty learning to read, share a common phonological weakness. A core phonological deficit exists in nearly all poor readers (Stanovich, 1992; Torgesen, 1999). Research has shown that phonological processing is the most prominent and enduring weakness in people with reading and spelling problems.

According to Stanovich (1992) the identification of the role of phonological processing in the earliest stages of reading acquisition is a notable scientific success story. One of the most exciting findings from recent research is that children's phonological awareness skills are relatively simple to teach. Increases in phonological awareness skill development result in improved literacy and language skills in young children (e.g., Ball & Blachman, 1988; Byrne & Fielding-Barnsely, 1995; Gillon, 2004; Lonigan, 2006).

Developmentally Appropriate Practice in Early Literacy

With all the focus on early literacy and early intervention, there sometimes are misperceptions and misinterpretations of what is appropriate and what we should expect young children to learn. In a collaborative effort, the National Association for the Education of Young Children (NAEYC) and the International Reading Association (IRA) have identified two essential areas of knowledge for early childhood educators as being necessary to support literacy development in young children. The first area is knowledge about the processes of literacy, and the second area is knowledge of the developmental sequences of children's learning that lead to competency in reading and writing (Neuman, Copple, & Bredekamp, 2000).

In a joint position statement on early literacy, the NAEYC and the IRA describe **developmentally appropriate practices** in reading and writing (Bredekamp & Copple, 1998) to include teaching approaches that consider:

- knowledge of the sequences of child development, learning to set achievable and challenging goals for literacy learning, and planning and using teaching strategies that vary with age and experience of the learners;
- an ongoing assessment procedure that identifies individual children's progress in literacy in order to plan successive lessons or to adapt instruction when children do not make expected progress or are at advanced levels; and
- an understanding of social and cultural contexts that affect how children make sense of their learning experiences in relation to what they already know and are able to do.

Our perception or feeling of how literacy develops impacts the way we plan and implement early literacy activities. It is important to identify our own perception of literacy development in young children to see if we have a blended approach.

Exercise 1.6 — Rate Your Current Beliefs

- Read each statement and indicate the number value as expressed in this scale that best represents your feelings or what you believe about children's literacy development.

   1 = strongly disagree   **2** = disagree   **3** = undecided   **4** = agree   **5** = strongly agree

   ___ 1. In order to learn to read, a child needs to know letter names and letter sounds.

   ___ 2. Becoming literate is a continuous, developmental process that begins very early in life.

   ___ 3. Early reading and writing practices exhibited by children result from direct exposure and guidance.

   ___ 4. To become literate, young children must have many and varied opportunities to read and write.

   ___ 5. The teaching of literacy must be systematic and sequential in operation.

   ___ 6. Reading and writing activities should be provided throughout the school day in all areas of curriculum.

   ___ 7. Reading includes the mechanical skill of turning printed symbols into sounds that are language.

   ___ 8. Play is one of the ways for young children to learn about written language.

   Add the number values of statements 1, 3, 5, and 7. _____

   Add the number values of statements 2, 4, 6, and 8. _____

In *Exercise 1.6*, the odd-numbered statements are often attributed to what is called a *skill-emphasis perspective*, or an *evidence-based reading research* (EBRR) *perspective*, and the even-numbered statements to an *emergent literacy perspective*. The EBRR perspective focuses on a core set of knowledge and skills that young children must develop to become successful readers and writers along with the strategies that can be used to teach these skills through explicit and direct instruction (Vukelich & Christie, 2004). The emergent literacy perspective places high value on the social and meaning-based aspects of literacy and creating a learning environment in which children can explore and learn.

In actuality, research supports all of the statements listed in *Exercise 6.1*. The term *blended* means that learning is teacher-led and skill-focused at times, as well as student-centered and creative. Both of these teaching methods can be meaningful, effective, engaging, and fun. Children who are not achieving developmental milestones are more likely to succeed with skill-focused early intervention. Do you have a *blended* approach?

By combining both EBRR and emergent literacy perspectives in early literacy instruction, we can identify eight basic principles (Vukelich & Christie, 2004, p. 14) supported by both the NAEYC and the IRA:

1. Early literacy and language instruction should focus on core content—the knowledge, skills, and dispositions that are predictive of later success in reading and writing.
2. Oral language lays the foundation for early literacy development.
3. Storybook-reading is a cornerstone of early literacy instruction.
4. A carefully planned classroom environment enables literacy development to flourish.
5. Children need opportunities to engage in emergent forms (i.e., activities that look like the adult form) of reading and writing.
6. Developmentally appropriate forms of direct instruction should be used to teach core literacy concepts and skills.
7. Teachers need to help parents support their children's language and literacy development.
8. Oral language and early literacy instruction and assessment should be guided by standards that define the knowledge and skills that young children will need to become successful readers and writers.

High ratings in both EBRR and emergent literacy perspectives represent a blended approach. Lower ratings in either perspective mean that the teaching strategies being used are not as effective in helping young children develop their literacy skills. In order for children to build these skills so vital to the literacy process, they need a blending of both creative and direct learning opportunities.

The results of the National Early Literacy Panel (NIFL, 2007) confirmed that oral language, phonological processing, and print knowledge are strongly predictive of how well young children will learn to read and write, and explicit and direct teaching is more likely to be effective than leaving growth to chance.

Wrap-Up

In this chapter, we identified oral language, phonological awareness, and print knowledge as foundations of early literacy. The skills in these areas are the building blocks for early reading and writing. Underlying abilities that influence both oral and written language are phonological processing and phonological representation. These skills work in an interconnected manner to process what is *said* and what is *read*. To facilitate early literacy skills in young children, early childhood educators must use developmentally appropriate and research-based practices. This includes an understanding of both literacy development and children's individual and cultural variations. As early childhood educators, we have a wonderful opportunity and an important responsibility to help young children develop the skills that will make their road to reading as successful as possible.

Reflection and Review

In small groups, discuss these questions:

1. What are the foundations of early literacy?
2. Describe the components of phonological processing.
3. Why is phonological processing important in oral language and written language development?
4. How does phonological representation impact oral and written language?
5. As you reflected on your perception of early literacy development (*Exercise 1.6*), did you have a stronger sense of one perspective more than the other (i.e., EBRR or emergent literacy), or did you consider both perspectives to be somewhat equally important?

Chapter 2: The Oral Language Connection to Literacy

This chapter describes: (a) the structures of oral language that provide the foundation for literacy; (b) the developmental sequences of how young children learn these structures; and (c) strategies that enhance oral language skills, including language-stimulation techniques, scaffolding, questioning strategies, and dialogic reading.

Learner Objectives for Chapter 2
- Describe the structural components of oral language.
- Describe the stages of oral and written language development.
- Compare the developmental stages and characteristics of oral and written language.
- Describe strategies that facilitate oral language in young children.

Warm-Up
- What are your thoughts about these questions? Jot down a response for each.
    1. What stages do children go through as they learn to talk?
       _____
       _____

    2. What are the stages children go through when they learn to read and write?
       _____
       _____

    3. What are the common characteristics between the stages of oral and written language development?
       _____
       _____

    4. What are the two main groups of English speech sounds?
       _____

5. How many speech sounds does the English language have?

6. What do you understand about:
   - phonology?

   - morphology?

   - syntax?

7. What types of language-stimulation strategies are used to enhance young children's language skills?

8. What age-appropriate characteristics do we need to consider when asking young children questions?

9. What are *dialogic* reading strategies?

Structures of Oral Language

Learning to talk usually happens naturally for children by listening to and talking with those around them. As children develop, they have a nearly universal capacity to learn the language they hear and to use the sounds of that language in their own speech guided by adult interactions.

All languages are based on ruled-ordered systems that integrate the structures of phonology, semantics, morphology, syntax, and prosody. These structural components are the basis of written language as well (see *Table 2.1*). When learning to read and write, children rely on their ability to use and understand oral language structures. A child's difficulty in learning to read and write can involve any of the components of oral language. Problems can occur in the production, comprehension, and awareness of language at any level (i.e., sound, syllable, word, sentence, and/or discourse). Gaining a better understanding of the structures of our oral language gives us a deeper understanding of how literacy skills develop.

The Oral Language Connection to Literacy

Table 2.1 Rule-Ordered Systems of Languages

PHONOLOGY	the study of the *sound system* of a language; includes speech sounds and rules to put sounds together into meaningful words
SEMANTICS	the study of *word meaning*
MORPHOLOGY	the rules of *word formation*
SYNTAX	the rules of *word order* in grammatical form
PROSODY	the *expression* of speech, a component of pragmatic language

Phonology

Phonology is the study of the sound system of a language and the rules used to put sounds together to make words. The English language contains a defined set of *phonemes* (speech sounds) consisting of vowels and consonants. In this context, consonants and vowels refer to *speech sounds*, not alphabet letters. Depending on geographic region, American English contains about 44 sounds (phonemes): 25 consonant sounds and 19 vowel sounds (Bauman-Waengler, 2009).

The phonological rule system of the English language has two important characteristics. First, because phonology is governed by rules, it is systematic and predictable. Second, the rules create a rhythm and redundancy, which facilitate learning and listening to English (Pinker, 1994).

When listening to connected speech, vowels provide the foundation for speech intelligibility. A perfect illustration is listening to the "speech" of a parrot saying, "Ah-ee, a-ah, a-ah," and we "hear," "Polly wants a cracker." Vowels are *open sounds*, which require only limited constriction of the mouth and articulators (i.e., tongue, lips, teeth), reducing the contrast in their pronunciations. (Think of the minimal difference between the short **e** and short **i** sounds.) Vowel sounds are made by moving your tongue in the front, middle, and back parts of your mouth and by the placement of your tongue from high to low. Lip movement helps to shape vowel sounds from rounded to unrounded positions. *Figure 2.1* (next page) illustrates vowel-sound mouth/articulator placement and lists sample words for each vowel-sound pronunciation. The *schwa* vowel is an unstressed, or unaccented, syllable, such as the first sound in the word **about** or in the second syllable of the word **carrot**. The /oi/ and /ou/ sounds are *diphthongs*, which are vowels that are produced with tongue and lip movement. The /er/, /ar/, and /or/ sounds are **r**-controlled vowels.

E-I-E-I-O! I know my vowels!

Figure 2.1 English Vowel Phonemes by Order of Articulation
(Adapted from Moats, 2009b)

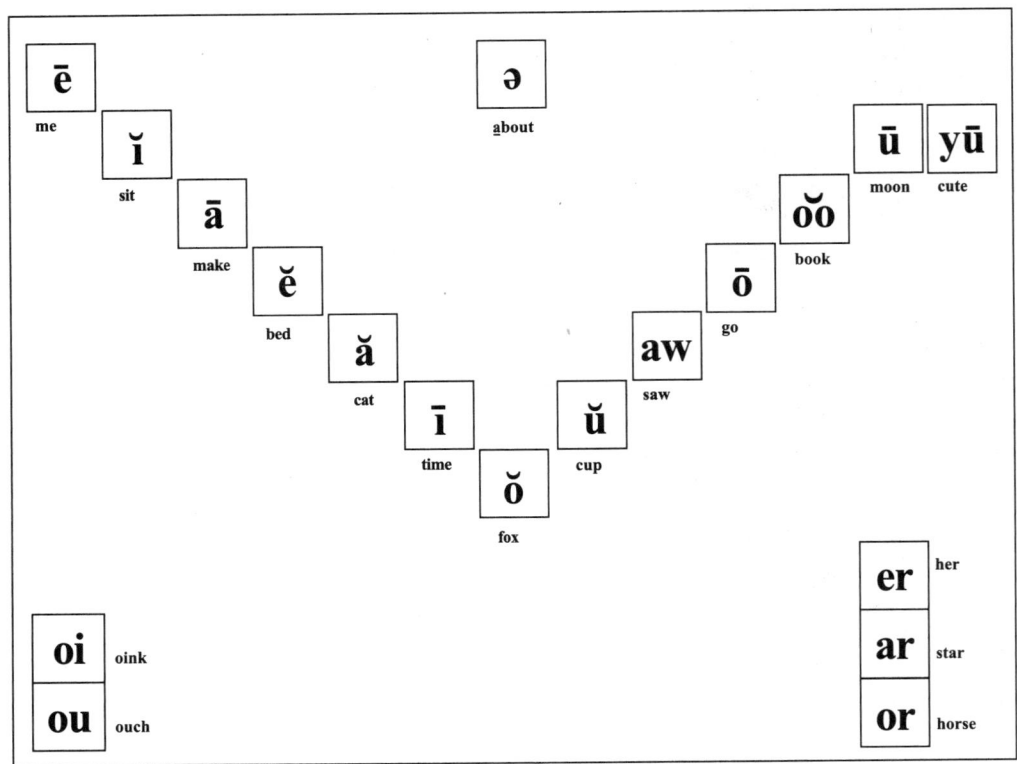

Young children generally learn to say vowel sounds easily in their speech; however, learning about vowels in written language may be a greater challenge. In kindergarten, typical phonics lessons often begin with short vowel sounds, such as in the words **hat**, **hen**, **hit**, **hot**, and **hut**. But there is no clear connection between the short vowel *sound* and the *letter name*. In written language, vowels have the most variation in how they are used and pronounced in words. And, the terms *short vowel sounds* and *long vowel sounds* do not adequately describe the perceived length of the sound as you say it.

Consonants are "closed" sounds, which are produced with some constriction of the mouth and a variety of movements of the articulators (i.e., tongue, lips, teeth, roof of mouth, back of throat). Consonant sounds add to the distinctness of speech intelligibility.

The Oral Language Connection to Literacy

Exercise 2.1 — Singing With Vowels and Consonants

- Sing the alphabet song saying only the vowel sounds in the syllables; for example, sing, "ā, ē, ē, ē" for "a, b, c, d." (Be careful to not "close" your mouth with your tongue or jaw.) Listen to the vowel sounds you are singing. What vowel sounds do you hear the most?

  _____

- Now sing the song again, this time with only the consonant sounds in the syllables; for example, sing, "__, /b/, /s/, /d/" for "a, b, c, d."

- Which version was easier to understand: the vowel or the consonant version?

  _____

Consonant Characteristics: Place, Manner, and Voicing

Consonant sounds have characteristics that include:
- **place** (*where* sounds are made—in the front, middle, or back of the mouth);
- **manner** (*how* sounds are formed with lips, teeth, tongue, or vocal tract); and
- **voicing** (whether a sound is *voiced* or *voiceless*).

Elements within these characteristics make some consonant sounds more perceptible than others. This is valuable information for effectively structuring activities to enhance the early literacy skills of young children when teaching them about letter names and the speech sounds that the letters represent.

Place: The place characteristic describes where consonant sounds are made in the mouth and what articulators (i.e., lips, tongue, teeth, roof of mouth) are used to produce them.

Lips	/p/, /b/, /m/, /f/, /v/, /w/, /wh/
Between teeth	/th/ (as in **thumb**), /th/ (as in **the**)
Behind top teeth	/t/, /d/, /n/, /l/, /s/, /z/
Roof of mouth	/sh/, /zh/, /ch/, /j/, /r/, /y/
Back of mouth	/k/, /g/, /ng/
Way in back of mouth	/h/

Exercise 2.2 — Evaluate Consonant Sounds

- Review and say aloud all of the consonant sounds as previously listed.
- Which consonant sounds are most perceptible?

  _____

  _____

LETRS® for Early Childhood Educators

Manner: The manner characteristic describes the way that consonant sounds are said or produced. There are five types of manner characteristics:

Stops	/p/, /b/, /t/, /d/, /ch/, /j/, /k/, /g/
Fricatives	/f/, /v/, /th/, /th̲/, /s/, /z/, /sh/, /zh/, /h/
Nasals	/m/, /n/, /ng/
Glides	/w/, /y/, /wh/
Liquids	/l/, /r/

Stop sounds are short in duration, and they "pop" out of the mouth with a puff of air.

Fricative sounds can be held or blown out for as long as your breath allows. As the term implies, friction is created by air being forced through the mouth.

Nasal sounds are the only sounds that use the nasal passageway for resonance. When you put your finger on the bridge of your nose while saying the /m/ sound, you should feel your nose vibrate. These sounds also last as long as breath is released.

Glide sounds and *liquid phonemes* are produced with some movement of either the lips or the tongue. The consonant glides /w/, /y/, and /h/ exist only *before* vowels, never after. Spellings such as **ow** in **snow** and **oy** in **boy** do not represent consonant glides. The letters **w** and **y** in those words are part of a vowel team spelling in which the letter combination represents one vowel sound, not a consonant. The liquid sounds /r/ and /l/ are pronounced differently depending on their position in a word and the sounds that surround them. For example, the /r/ in **red** is different than the /r/ in **core**; the /l/ in **lock** is not spoken the same way as the /l/ in **doll**. When /l/ or /r/ come at the end of a syllable or a word, the phonemes may become blended with the preceding vowel (e.g., /ar/, /or/, /er/).

Exercise 2.3 — Select a Sound for Instruction

- When designing an activity for young children that focuses on isolating beginning sounds in words, which of these two sounds are more perceptible, or easier, for children to hear when considering manner or how sounds are produced?
  - ○ Identifying the /t/ in the word **top**
  - ○ Identifying the /s/ sound in the word **sun**

Voicing: The *voicing* characteristic contrasts *voiceless* consonant sounds (produced without vibrating the vocal folds in the larynx, or voice box) and *voiced* consonant sounds (produced by vibrating the vocal folds). Place your hand on your larynx and say, "Ah." Do you feel it vibrate? That means your voice is "on." All vowels are voiced sounds, while some consonants are voiced and some are voiceless.

Several pairs of consonant sounds, called *cognates*, are produced in the same place and in the same manner, but one sound of the pair is voiceless and the other sound is voiced (see *Table 2.2*). Say the /s/ sound while feeling your larynx and concentrating on where your tongue is. Now say the /z/ sound. Did your tongue do anything differently? What about your larynx? Try this with each cognate pair: /p/ and /b/; /f/ and /v/; /th/ and /th̲/; /t/ and /d/; /s/ and /z/; /sh/ and /zh/; /ch/ and /j/; /k/ and /g/; and /wh/ and /w/.

The Oral Language Connection to Literacy

Table 2.2 Voiced and Voiceless Consonant Cognates

Voiceless	/p/	/f/	/th/	/t/	/s/	/sh/	/ch/	/k/	/wh/	/h/
Voiced	/b/	/v/	/<u>th</u>/	/d/	/z/	/zh/	/j/	/g/	/w/	/y/, /w/, /l/, /r/, /m/, /n/, /ng/

One additional voiceless sound is /h/. The remaining voiced consonant sounds are glides /y/ and /w/, liquids /l/ and /r/, and nasals /m/, /n/, and /ng/.

Exercise 2.4 Consonant Sounds With Voicing

- Which consonant sounds must be pronounced with voicing or vocalization?

_____

_____

The sounds of English provide the building blocks for the words we say. General milestones for speech-sound development include:
- 2-year-olds should say words with some semblance to the standard form.
- 3-year-olds should be understood by those who are familiar with them.
- 4-year-olds should be generally understood by others, and may still be learning to correctly say sounds such as /r/, /l/, /th/, /sh/, and ch/.
- 5-year-olds should be understood by others while still learning to correctly say the sounds /r/ and /th/.

The sounds of our language also provide the building blocks for the words we read and write.
- How many letters do we have in our alphabet?
- How many phonemes do we have in our language?

With 26 alphabet letters and 40-some phonemes in the English language, we do not always have a direct match between letters and speech sounds. Our written language uses a variety of letter patterns to represent speech sounds and, because of multiple influences from other languages, English has many letter patterns or spellings for the 40-some speech sounds.

One important skill associated with early reading is being able to attend to the speech sounds in words and isolate them. This is an important phonemic awareness skill, which will be discussed in Chapter 3. For our purpose here, it is vital that early childhood educators be able to attend to the speech sounds in words in order to be able to teach children this task. In *Exercise 2.5*, identify how many speech sounds each written word comprises. Make sure you listen to the speech sounds, and do not be influenced by the letters of the written word.

Exercise 2.5 — Phonemic Awareness: Count the Phonemes

- Identify and count the number of speech sounds in these words.

Word	Identity of sounds	Number of sounds
string		
joyless		
dodge		
mixed		
heard		
crash		
though		
chew		
house		
quiet		

Spanish Phonology

In general, the phonology of Spanish is simpler than that of English because Spanish has fewer consonant and vowel sounds. There are consonant sounds in Spanish that do not exist in English, and vice versa. Depending on the dialect, most phoneticians agree that Spanish has 21 phonemes: 16 consonant sounds, including two glides (also called *semivowels*), and only five vowel sounds (Moats, 2009b). Spanish does not contain the English consonant sounds /th/, /th/, /v/, /z/, /sh/, /zh/, or /j/, or consonant blends with the /s/ sound. Therefore, Spanish speakers may pronounce these English words as follows:

English	Spanish
thing	sing
that	dat
TV	TB
zoo	soo
shoe	choe
garage	garach
judge	chudge
school	eschool

LETRS® for Early Childhood Educators

AAE Phonological Patterns

African American English (AAE) has predictable phonological patterns that differ from standard American English (SAE). These variations affect speech production and sentence patterns, including:
- Variations on /th/ and /th/ sounds:
  — initial /th/ pronounced with /f/ (*free* for **three**);
  — initial /th/ pronounce with /d/ (*dere* for **there**);
  — medial /th/ pronounced with /d/ (*moder* for **mother**); and
  — final /th/ pronounced with /f/ (*wif* for **with**)
- Deleting or softening /l/ and /r/ after vowels:
  — *baw* for **ball**; *hamma* for **hammer**

These are only a few of the pattern differences between AAE and SAE. This dialect is a good example of the dynamic nature of language and the variations and influences that occur when cultures are blended over time.

Semantics

The second oral language structure is **semantics**, the study of word meaning and vocabulary development. We typically learn words at a receptive level (i.e., what we understand) before we are able to say them at an expressive level. Vocabulary development is vital to comprehension of both oral and written language. Young children learn words at an amazing rate. Beginning at about 24 months of age and lasting through the preschool years, children demonstrate a phenomenon called "fast mapping" in which they can learn the meanings of new words very rapidly, with just a few exposures (Gopnik et al., 1999).

Table 2.3 lists the average number of *expressive* vocabulary words children typically have learned to say at different ages (McLaughlin, 1998).

Table 2.3 Expressive Vocabulary Timeline of Young Children

Age	Number of words
12 months	First word
18 months	50
24 months	200–300
3 years	900–1,000
5 years	2,100–2,200

General estimates of receptive language at varying ages can be obtained by multiplying levels of expressive language by about four times. Vocabulary grows as children's understanding of their world increases within their everyday routines and experiences. They develop the ability to categorize and classify words, thereby creating an organization for storing the things they know.

Categories can be based on groups such as animals, food, clothes, and transportation, and on attributes such as color and size. Children learn relational terms such as *before/after*, *since*, *until*; opposites such as *big/little*, *long/short*, *heavy/light*; location words and phrases such as *under*, *next to*, *behind*, *in front*; and words related to their families, such as *sister*, *brother*, etc. A major advancement in preschool vocabulary development is children's ability to use *decontextualized language*, which refers to talking about something outside of the here and now or not in the present context, such as describing something that happened last week.

Phonological representation is an important aspect of vocabulary development. In order to be able to say a word, you need to be able to "hear" it in your mind (your inner speech), and in order to develop your inner speech, you need to hear words over and over in meaningful contexts to understand what the words mean. The number of words young children hear in their environments is significantly correlated to academic success (Hart & Risley, 1995).

Exercise 2.6 List Vocabulary Words in a Storybook

- Look through the text of a children's book that you use in your setting. (A good example is *The Mitten* by Jan Brett.)
- Make a list of the vocabulary words that may be unfamiliar to the children in your setting. How many words did you identify?

_____   _____   _____

_____   _____   _____

_____   _____   _____

_____   _____   _____

Exercise 2.6 highlights the value of using children's storybooks as a means of exposing children to rich vocabulary. Children's books are one of the best sources of unfamiliar and rare words for young children, and the exposure seems to "prime" their brains for learning more words (Wolfe & Nevills, 2004). Because of the innate value of this dynamic process, reading the same book repeatedly to young children is not only important but also necessary.

Morphology

Morphology is the study and description of word formation. We can change word forms (i.e., parts of speech) by adding prefixes and suffixes, which also changes the word meaning and use. Each word and word part that adds meaning is considered a *morpheme*, such as plural markers in **hat<u>s</u>** and **dresse<u>s</u>** and verb endings like **jump<u>s</u>, jump<u>ed</u>, jump<u>ing</u>**. A morpheme may be a single sound that represents a word (e.g., the personal pronoun **I**), or a morpheme may have multiple sounds and syllables (e.g., **enamel**). The word **enamel** is one morpheme with three syllables, whereas the word **rewriting** has three morphemes and three syllables (**re-writ[e]-ing**).

Morphology is an important structural component of our oral language. As part of our language experience, we subconsciously learn specific linguistic rules. For example, we say, "He *went* … ," but young children often say, "He *goed* … ," because they have not yet learned the underlying rule for the past tense of the verb **go**. We use our phonological processing and "inner speech" (i.e., how words sound within our phonological representation) when speaking and can tell that a word form or sentence does not sound right.

Exercise 2.7 Add Morphological Endings

- Following predictable, structural rules, the word **talk** may have many different endings (i.e., morphemes) that change the form of the word.
- Add each morpheme below to the word **talk**, and then note the word's part of speech (e.g., noun, verb, adjective).

Morpheme	Part of speech
-s	_____
-er	_____
-ed	_____
-ing	_____
-ative	_____
-tion	_____

Let's review the answers to *Exercise 2.7*:
- When **-s, -er, -ing,** and **-ative** are added to the base word **talk**, all forms follow expected word patterns and structures.
- When **-ed** is added to **talk**, what is the final sound? It is pronounced *talkt*, not *talk-ed*. The word **talked** has only *one* syllable but *two* morphemes, or meaningful parts!
- When **-tion** is added to **talk** (*talktion*), it is immediately clear that **-tion** does not work, and a morphologic rule has been broken. Consider this: All of the morphemes (or forms of the morphemes) listed in this exercise work with the word **act**, making **act<u>s</u>, act<u>or</u>, act<u>ed</u>, act<u>ing</u>, act<u>ive</u>,** and **act<u>ion</u>**. So why doesn't **-tion** work with **talk**? Because **talk** is an Anglo-Saxon word, and **-tion** is a Latin morpheme. We can add a *Latin ending* to a *Latin word* (in this case, **act**) but not to an Anglo-Saxon word.

I am coloring and scissoring.

The ability to detect an error when saying *talktion* and knowing that *-ed* is pronounced as /t/ in **talked** results from our experience with and our underlying understanding of English language rules and what "sounds" right. The important point is that we rely on our underlying understanding of the rules that govern our language when listening, speaking, reading, and writing, even if we do not consciously know the specific linguistic rule.

One difference between oral language and written language is how syllables in words are divided when they are *said* as opposed to when they are *written*. In spoken language, we segment words into syllables following phonological rules and patterns. A phonological pattern in English is a preference to end syllables with a vowel and to start syllables with a consonant. For example, when we say the word **leader**, we say *lea-* for the first syllable and *-der* for the second syllable; for the word **basket**, we say *ba-sket*. Each first syllable ends with a vowel, and the second syllable begins with a consonant or consonant blend.

Exercise 2.8 Divide Words by Syllables and Morphemes

- Divide these words into syllable units and morpheme units.

Word	Syllable division	Morpheme division
reader		
hats		
rented		
underplayed		
kangaroo		
biography		

Let's review the answers to *Exercise 2.8*:

An underlying phonological rule pattern or preference of English is to start words or syllables with a consonant sound.

The Oral Language Connection to Literacy

- When you divide the word **reader** into syllables, the second syllable begins with the /d/ sound (**rea-der**); however, the morphemes are **read** and **er**.
- The word **hats** has one syllable but two morphemes (**hat** + **-s**).
- The second syllable of **rented** is **ted** and the second morpheme is **-ed**.
- The word **underplayed** has three syllables (**un-der-played**) and three morphemes (**under-play-ed**).
- The word **kangaroo** has three syllables (**kan-ga-roo**) but one morpheme.
- The word **biography** has four syllables (**bi-o-gra-phy**) but three morphemes (**bio-graph-y**).

When these words are written, we divide them in different ways following orthographic and morphologic rules (see *Table 2.4*). This written information helps us understand how to read words based on syllable types.

Table 2.4 Summary of Six Types of Syllables in Written English

Syllable Type	Syllable Definition	Word Examples
Closed	Ends with a consonant, making the vowel short.	**pet, cat**
Open	Ends with a vowel, making the vowel long.	**he, ri-pen**
Consonant **-le**	/l/ serves as the vowel sound.	**ap-ple, ta-ble**
Vowel team	Combinations of vowel letters that represent long, short, or diphthong vowel sounds.	**eat, boat, sigh, boil**
Vowel **-r**	/r/ acts as part of the vowel.	**fir, star**
Vowel-Consonant-**e**	Widely known as the "Silent-**e** Rule."	**game, time**

See LETRS Module 3 (Moats, 2009c) for a more detailed description of the six syllable types of written English.

Exercise 2.9 | Locate Morphemes

- Using the same children's book you reviewed in *Exercise 2.6* (page 28), list the various suffix morphemes that appear in the text.

_____   _____   _____   _____

_____   _____   _____   _____

_____   _____   _____   _____

_____   _____   _____   _____

Highlighting how morphemes change the meanings and forms of words helps children expand their vocabulary. Think of how children learn the words **eat**, **eats**, **eating**, and **eater**. How do we help them understand these distinctions?

Syntax

Syntax (commonly known as *grammar*) refers to the set of rules used to put words into sentences in the proper order. Again, there are many linguistic rules that dictate the order of words in sentences. These rules build on phonology, semantics, and morphology. The following groups of words may be reordered to make sentences. It does not take long to place them in the correct order.

Group 1: shoe her lost Cinderella
Group 2: injured was the driver
Group 3: flashlight your where is

This task is easy because we have a strong underlying understanding of the syntactic rule system of English. Most likely, the words are rearranged with the subject noun first, followed by the verb or action, and then the object noun: "<u>Cinderella</u> (subject noun) <u>lost</u> (verb) her <u>shoe</u> (object noun)." This particular pattern is the most prevalent structure in our language (Pinker, 1994), although it is possible to reorder the words to create another sentence: "Her shoe, Cinderella lost." While this sentence is syntactically correct, this structure (object, subject, verb) is not as common. How can the words in the next two groups be arranged to make a sentence?

Young children usually demonstrate characteristics of general sentence structure development combining syntax and morphology as follows:

- 2-year-olds start putting words together in short phrases.
- 3-year-olds use three- to six-word sentences and add word endings like **-s**, **-ing**, and **-ed**.
- 4-year-olds string many words together and combine sentences related to the same topic.
- 5-year-olds carry on conversations with mostly grammatically correct sentence forms.

Exercise 2.10 Quantify Sentence Length

- Using the same children's book as in *Exercise 2.9*, identify the longest sentence in the text. How many words does the sentence have?

_____

Many children's books have sentences that are quite long and much more complex than young children are able to comprehend. Repeated readings help children build an understanding of sentence structure because multiple exposures provide opportunities to process and untangle sentence structures that are more common in written language than in spoken language.

Prosody

Prosody refers to the expression we use when we talk and read aloud and includes the rhythm and melody of speech production. It is a component of pragmatic language, the way we use language to communicate. The meaning of what we say is affected not only by the words we use but also in the way we say them. The expression used while speaking and reading aloud helps in understanding what we hear and comprehending what we read.

Exercise 2.11 — Experiment With Prosodic Stress

- Say each sentence a few times, placing stress on the underlined words in the sentences.
- Describe the different meanings that are conveyed based on the word stress.

1. She got a <u>pink slip</u>.

2. I saw a <u>man eating shark</u>.

3. She fed <u>her dog bones</u>.

Let's review *Exercise 2.11*. Depending on word stress:
- The first sentence conveys that a woman either lost her job or bought an underwear item.
- The second sentence conveys either a gentleman having an exotic dinner or a sighting of an ominous sea creature.
- The third sentence conveys one of three possibilities about the girl's actions: (1) She is serving bones to a female visitor or a female dog; (2) She is giving her dog something to eat; or (3) She is feeding her dog named Bones.

This exercise clearly illustrates that language meaning or intent is directly affected by different oral stress expressions (i.e., prosodic differences). It drives home the point that the expression we use when talking and reading aloud to children promotes their language development and helps them more accurately comprehend what we express.

Because expression must be inferred in written language and construed by the reader as part of the reading process, the absence of prosody in print may create multiple possible meanings for what is read, which can impact comprehension. Therefore, when reading books to (and with) young children, it is important to use a lot of expression and animation in our voices to provide prosodic cues to convey the meaning of what we are reading.

These five structural components of oral language—phonology, semantics, morphology, syntax, and prosody—constitute the foundation of written language. Each component develops in an interrelated manner, building skills from simple to more complex, as children learn to talk. Children learn about the processes of early reading and writing using their understanding of oral language.

Typical Developmental Stages of Oral and Written Language

A striking parallel exists between the stages of learning oral language and the stages of learning literate, or written, language. The ways that children learn to speak and listen are similar to the ways they learn to read and write (Paulson et al., 2001); each level of development shares a similar path of acquisition and competence. Engaging children in developmentally appropriate activities that focus on both spoken and written language tends to produce improved skill and mastery in both language forms.

Stage 1 (Oral: Prelexic) (Written: Prelogographic)

Prelexic	Prelogographic
Babies	Toddlers to preschool

The first stage of language and literacy development occurs *before* a symbolic relationship is established in the form of spoken words or print. The **prelexic** oral language stage is commonly referred to as "cooing and babbling." These vocalizations, which have a sound structure but no meaning, are crucial to the development of phonological processing.

The **prelogographic** literacy stage exists in very young children, when they have no awareness or understanding of print symbols they see in their environment (Snowling & Stackhouse, 1996).

How old are children when they recognize the golden arches? At this point, they have moved into the next stage of literacy development, which is characterized by visual understanding of symbols in their environment.

Stage 2 (Oral: Lexic) (Written: Logographic, or Prealphabetic)

Lexic	Logographic (Prealphabetic)
Toddlers	Preschool to kindergarten

Both language and literacy in the second developmental stage are characterized by simple *whole-word structures* and *print representations*. Around their first birthday, babies associate something important from their routines and experiences with a sequence of sounds. At this age, they say their first words, entering the **lexic** stage of oral language development. For example, when a baby says "Da!" as the family dog enters the room, that single word communicates the whole message: "I see a dog!"

When children recognize written symbols in their environment (e.g., the logo of their favorite restaurant) they merge into the **logographic**, or **prealphabetic**, stage of literacy development (Ehri, 1996). Children understand print symbols as whole entities; the parts carry no significance. They recognize words by visual characteristics without understanding that letters represent speech sounds (Moats, 2000; Schickedanz, 1999; Snowling & Stackhouse, 1996).

> Sharing a lesson about being a good helper with a group of preschool children, the teacher held up a poster bearing the words "Good Helping Kids" from the book *Good Talking Words* (Paulson & van den Pol, 1998).
>
> A 4-year-old boy, Gary, jumped up in an excited manner with a revelation. He pointed to the poster and said, "That's my name!"
>
> The teacher pointed to the word **Good** on the poster and asked Gary if he had a "G" in his name. He responded, "No!" He then pointed to the "G" again and repeated, "That's my name!"
>
> Gary recognized the first letter in his name and in the word **Good**. That single visual component—the capital letter **G**—was what imparted meaning to him.

Stage 3 (Oral: Systematic Simplification) (Written: Early Alphabetic)

Systematic Simplification	Early Alphabetic
Toddlers to preschool	Late preschool to kindergarten

Oral language and literacy structures used by children in the third developmental stage are **systematic simplifications** of standard oral and written language structures. In this stage of language development, children have developed a vocabulary of about 50 words, and they begin to combine words into simple sentences. These sentences contain simplified sound structures and word-order structures. For example, a child who says, "No go," conveys the meaning, "I don't want to go," or "du peas," for "I want some juice, please."

In the **early alphabetic** stage, children begin to develop a simple understanding of the alphabetic principle. They realize that letters of the alphabet represent speech sounds in the words they say, hear, and see (Moats, 2000). They create *temporary spellings* of the words they write, using a simplified structure (e.g., *lv* for **love**; *wn* for **one**; *da* for **day**). The "early alphabetic" label can be somewhat confusing because, at this stage, children are learning more than only the letters of the alphabet; they are also learning letter-sound relationships.

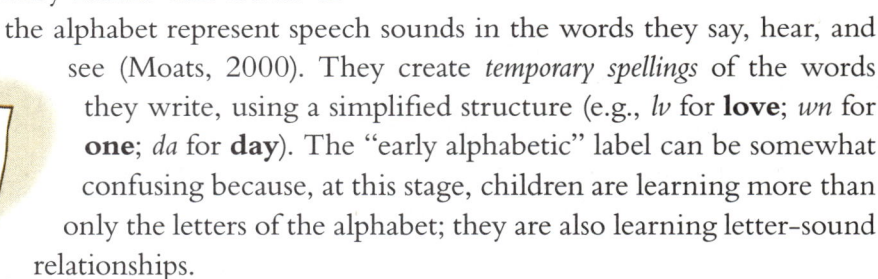

Stage 4 (Oral: Assembly)
(Written: Later Alphabetic)

Assembly	Later Alphabetic
Preschool	Kindergarten to early elementary

The fourth stage of oral language and literacy development is characterized by a *developing awareness* of the structures of oral and written language. The **assembly** stage of language development begins as children use more words in their sentences and add endings (e.g., **-s** for plurals and possessives; **-ed** for past tense; **-ing**) to their words. Children are developing an awareness of the sentence structure of oral language (e.g., "Me goed to a store" and "What you are doing?"). Later in this stage, their sentences become longer and more grammatically correct.

In literacy, the **later alphabetic** stage occurs as children develop an increased awareness and a better understanding of the alphabetic principle. They are learning to associate letters with sounds and are able to decode, or sound out, simple words (e.g., **go**, **cat**, **pop**). Children also are developing the skills to spell phonetically (e.g., *luv* for **love**; *tabl* for **table**). Familiar words that children repeatedly encounter become part of their visual memory and are easily identified as sight words (Moats, 2000; Schickedanz, 1999).

Stage 5 (Oral: Metaphonological)
(Written: Consolidated Alphabetic)

Metaphonological	Consolidated Alphabetic
Preschool	Elementary grades on up

The final stage of both language and literacy development is characterized by an ability to *manipulate the structures* of oral and written language. Children in the **metaphonological** stage of language development can consciously (meta-) realize that the words they use to communicate not only have a *meaning* but also a *structure* that can be changed and manipulated.

Figure 2.2 summarizes the typical developmental stages of oral and written language acquisition, beginning from shortly after birth.

Figure 2.2 The Five Developmental Stages of Oral and Written Language

Language Development	YEARS	Literacy Development
1. **Prelexic** (cooing and babbling) 0-1 years	0	1. **Prelogographic** (before symbols) 0–2½ years
2. **Lexic** (whole oral words) 1–1½ years	1	
3. **Systematic Simplification** (word combinations) 1½–2½ years	2	2. **Logographic/Prealphabetic** (whole written word) 2½–4 years
4. **Assembly** (syllable combinations) 2½–3½ years	3	
5. **Metaphonological** (aware of word structure) 3–4 years	4	3. **Early Alphabetic** (simple letter-sound correspondences) 4–5 years
	5	4. **Later Alphabetic** (phonetic spelling) 5–7 years
	6	
	7+	5. **Consolidated Alphabetic** (fluent reader) 7+ years

Exercise 2.12 | A Case Study

- Read this scenario, then reflect on the pertinent questions.

    In April of kindergarten, a girl was experiencing difficulty learning letter names and the associated sounds. The teacher wanted to know how the girl's phonemic awareness skills were developing. Using a sound-segmenting task, the teacher modeled how to segment the sounds in the word **cat** and then asked the girl to say the sounds in that word. She was successful in answering, "/k/ – /ă/ – /t/."

    The teacher then told the girl that the word **top** also has three sounds, and requested her to say the three sounds in that word. Thinking very hard, the girl responded with, "/k/ – /k/ – /k/."

    At this point, the teacher did not know if the girl did not understand the direction for the task or if she did not know how to isolate the sounds in words. The teacher again reviewed the sounds in the word **cat**. The student once again successfully answered, "/k/ – /ă/ – /t/."

    The teacher then presented the word **gum**, saying that **gum** has three sounds. She asked the girl to segment the word. This time, the girl replied, "Munch, munch, munch." Now, knowing what the girl's phonemic awareness skills were, the teacher presented the word **lake** for the girl to segment.

- What do you think the girl's response was? If you thought of something like, "Swish, swish, swish" or "Splash, splash, splash," you also were able to identify how this girl was thinking. She was thinking of the *sound* that the object words made, not the speech sounds in the words themselves. Can you imagine her confusion and lack of understanding of class discussions about letter names and the sounds that letters represent when her understanding of letters was nothing more than a series of squiggly lines? This girl was not representing the *structures* of the words; she was thinking of the *meanings*.
- What do you think about this girl's language development, especially at the metaphonological level?

In the *literacy orthographic*, or **consolidated alphabetic**, stage (Ehri, 1996), children recognize patterns and "chunks" of written language. Experienced readers see the suffix **-tion** and know it doesn't rhyme with **lion**, but sounds like *shun*; they see **-ight** and know it sounds like *ite*, not *ig het*; they say "talkt" and write **talked**. Experienced readers have an underlying understanding of the structure of the oral language system and an ability to apply that information to manipulate the structures of written language.

Traits and Implications of Developmental Difficulties

When children experience difficulty developing oral language, they often get "stuck" at the *systematic simplification* stage (Stage 3) of language development. They encounter difficulty learning the structure of language and may display underdeveloped sentence structures, limited vocabulary usage, and/or have speech that is difficult to understand. Children who struggle to acquire oral language often experience similar challenges in developing reading and writing skills (American Speech-Language-Hearing Association [ASHA], 2001).

When children have difficulty learning to read and write, they often get "stuck" at the *logographic/prealphabetic* stage of literacy development (Stage 2). They can recognize a few words by sight or as whole chunks (e.g., **stop**, **mom**, **dinosaur**), but they have not learned the relationship between letters and sounds and how the letters in words can be pulled apart and put back together to be read (Snowling & Stackhouse, 1996).

Families, caregivers, and early childhood educators have a significant impact on children's early language and literacy skills. A strong connection exists between the home and school literacy environments and children's language abilities (Whitehurst & Lonigan, 1998). Literacy development is affected by language and literacy experiences shared by family members and teachers, written material found in the home and at school, and the attitudes of the family and school toward literacy. Children who are provided with a wide variety of experiences and opportunities to talk, tell stories, read storybooks, draw, and write are generally successful in learning to read and write. Those who work with young children have a critical window of opportunity to offer support in helping them acquire rich language and emerging literacy skills.

Many skills learned during the preschool years lay the foundation for literacy development in elementary school. Adults who understand typical behavior and expected skill development, along with appropriate ways of stimulating language and literacy skills, can help children build a strong foundation in language and pave the way for success with literacy.

Strategies That Facilitate Oral Language Development

The amount and kind of talk that adults use with young children are highly predictive of important educational outcomes. Parents who are highly verbal with their children and who use affirming, supportive responses tend to have children with larger vocabularies (Hart & Risley, 1995) and more advanced language development (Gilkerson & Richards, 2008). The quality of adult-child conversations is as important as the quantity (Dickinson & Tabors, 2001).

Early childhood educators need to provide direct opportunities for interaction. During large-group activities (e.g., Circle time), we should lead conversations based on the planned activity content, provide new information connected to previous knowledge and experience, embed new or novel vocabulary, and ask structured questions to gauge children's understanding. During less structured times (e.g., free play), we can encourage children to extend their ideas, use new or novel vocabulary in conversations, and give every child an opportunity to share (Casey & Sheran, 2004). Quality interactions require the use of effective language-stimulation techniques.

Language-Stimulation Techniques

In order to become competent language users, young children need adults who intentionally use oral language-stimulation techniques when interacting with them. Traditional techniques often described in early childhood settings include:

- **Parallel talk**: An adult describes what the child is doing.
  Example: As children are arriving at school, an adult says, "You are unzipping your coat and putting it in your cubby."
- **Self-talk**: An adult talks about what he or she is doing, using short sentences.
  Example: At snack time, an adult says, "I am crushing up crackers and putting them in my chicken noodle soup."
- **Expansion**: An adult adds more information to the sentences that the child expresses.
  Example: A child says, "A fire truck!" An adult responds, "There is a big, yellow fire truck with a siren!"

Exercise 2.13 Expand Utterances

- Expand these children's responses:

  1. "Ball."

  2. "A dog a bone."

  3. "Her falled down."

  4. "He made a big bubble."

Focusing on the purpose of an adult-child conversation or exchange, Justice (2004) has identified three types of interactions (see *Table 2.5*, next page):

1. *Child-oriented* responses create and maintain a shared conversation.
2. *Interaction* responses encourage children to talk.
3. *Language-modeling* responses consist of adult demonstrations of word meaning (vocabulary), structure (morphology and syntax) and how language is used.

A blending of these types of responses should be used throughout the day in a variety of settings and situations.

Table 2.5 Three Types of Responses in Adult-Child Conversations

Child-Oriented Responses

- **Waiting**: The adult uses a slow pace during the conversation, listens actively to the child, and does not dominate the conversation.
- **Extending**: The adult repeats what the child says and adds a small amount of information.

Interaction Responses

- **Pausing**: The adult pauses expectantly and frequently during interactions to encourage turn-taking and participation.
- **Confirming**: The adult responds to the child's utterances by confirming an understanding of the child's intentions.
- **Imitating**: The adult repeats exactly (or paraphrases closely) what the child says.

Language-Modeling Responses

- **Labeling**: The adult provides labels for familiar and unfamiliar objects, actions, and concepts.
- **Scripting**: The adult provides a possible response for the child and engages the child in familiar routines.

Exercise 2.14 Match the Type of Response to the Sentence

- Match the type of interaction response to these sentences. (These examples might coincide with a play-dough tabletop activity.)

   a. Waiting   _____ 1. A child says, "I made a snake!" and the teacher responds, "Yes, you made a snake."

   b. Extending   _____ 2. A child says, "Look, I made a snake," and the teacher replies, "You made a long blue and green snake."

   c. Pausing   _____ 3. A child says, "Look, I made a snake," and the teacher replies, "You made a snake."

   d. Confirming   _____ 4. The teacher rolls out her play dough while watching the children and then comments, "I like rolling out play dough."

   e. Imitating   _____ 5. After using a tree-shaped cookie cutter, the teacher says, "Look, I made a yellow … " and waits for a response.

   f. Labeling   _____ 6. A child chooses a cookie cutter and the teacher says, "You are going to make a red triangle."

   g. Scripting   _____ 7. A child chooses a cookie cutter and the teacher says, "You are making a red triangle. Tell me what you are making."

The Oral Language Connection to Literacy

Another intentional instruction strategy to enhance children's learning is using the simple formula of "I Do It, We Do It, You Do It." This strategy involves having the adult model a concept, repeating the concept with the child, and then having the child say or perform the concept on his/her own. Encourage the "You Do It" step until the child has enough practice to establish the concept or skill.

Exercise 2.15 Practice Language Modeling

- Use language modeling responses and the "I Do It, We Do It, You Do It" technique in the following scenarios. (Scenario 1 provides suggestions for reference.)

Scenario 1: During free play, you are interacting with children who are building with blocks. One child says, "Me want that one."	
"I Do It" (adult models)	You might respond with a labeling technique by saying, "You want the big red block" and a scripting technique by saying, "Tell me, 'I want the big red block.'" If the child cannot say it on his or her own, then proceed to the next step.
"We Do It" (adult and child together)	Encourage the child to say along with you, "I want the big red block."
"You Do It" (child says it)	Have the child repeat the sentence on his/her own. Repeat the "You Do It" step as necessary.
Scenario 2: During a book-reading activity looking at big trucks and moving machines, a child points to a bulldozer but does not label it.	
"I Do It"	
"We Do It"	
"You Do It"	
Scenario 3: At a tabletop activity glueing shapes onto a piece of paper, one child grabs the glue from another child who, in turn, hits the grabber. What techniques would you use for the grabber and the hitter?	
"I Do It"	
"We Do It"	
"You Do It"	

Scaffolding Strategies

Scaffolding is a technique to foster children's language development by encouraging them to perform at progressively higher levels, first with assistance and later independently. Language scaffolds should be incorporated into language-stimulation techniques when talking to children in everyday conversations to help them expand and reinforce their oral language skills.

Literacy scaffolds can also be incorporated into reading and writing activities to help children develop an understanding of the meaning and function of print in texts such as stories, poems, reports, and recipes. Scaffolds may be removed once children are able to participate without them. *Table 2.6* lists read-aloud scaffolding techniques often used by adults when reading storybooks to children (Kaderavek & Sulzby, 1998).

Table 2.6 Read-Aloud Scaffolding Techniques

Labeling and commenting	The adult reader looks at and points to pictures in books and talks about them (e.g., "There's a ball. It's yellow.").
Verbal dialogue about a picture or storyline	The adult reader creates stories about pictures or provides a storyline with only pictures (e.g., "The dog is jumping. He wants a bone.").
Pauses	The adult reader has the child fill in words in stories the child knows or has the child anticipate what will come next in a story (e.g., in the book *Brown Bear, Brown Bear* by Bill Martin Jr., say, "I see a red bird looking at _____.").
Sentence recasting	The adult reader reads the storyline and then repeats it to help the child understand or comprehend a sentence or phrase (e.g., the question "Brown bear, brown bear, what do you see?" is repeated to provide verbal support, or the adult can use gestures along with the recast to enhance understanding).
Reading text with syntax simplification	When sentence structure is too difficult for the child, the adult reader simplifies the sentence (e.g., "The sparrows implored Peter Rabbit to exert himself" becomes "The birds told Peter to try harder").

Tag questions	This technique is used frequently in conversations with children and, to some extent, helps bridge children's understanding to gain agreement (e.g., the adult asks, "That's a dog, *isn't it?*" or "He likes red cars, *doesn't he?*").
Direct questions	Direct questions are used to provide the adult with information about what the child understands (e.g., the adult asks, "What is she doing?" or "What color is that?").
Story retelling	The adult reader summarizes the story and encourages the child to retell the story (e.g., a child's retelling may be, "Peter got stuck in the garden and almost got caught").

Exercise 2.16 Practice Scaffolding

- Choose a children's storybook that you like to read. On different pages:

1. Label a picture and make a comment about it.
2. Make up a story about the picture.
3. Read part of the text, then pause to let children fill in the word or words.
4. Read another sentence, then rephrase it using fewer words and simpler vocabulary.
5. Make a comment about the text, and include a tag question.
6. Create a direct question about the text.
7. Summarize the story by retelling it.

Questioning Strategies

Questioning strategies are an important aspect of adult interactions with children. A continuum of questioning strategies ranges from simple recall questions to those that require some type of evaluation or rating. Context is another aspect that needs to be considered in questioning routines. Questions that pertain to the present or immediate context are typically easier than those that relate to something that is not in the present. For example, when looking at a book, you might ask a child a question about the color of a house on a page (immediate context) and then ask the child about the color of his/her house (non-immediate context). When interacting with children, be sure to use a range of progressively sophisticated questioning strategies:

- **Recall** questions require a response that labels, matches, and recalls information.
- **Application** questions describe something that happens.
- **Analysis** questions require an answer that summarizes or compares information.

- **Synthesis** requires combining information from different sources in order to respond.
- **Evaluation** questions involve a rating or judgment.

Figure 2.3 Question Hierarchy

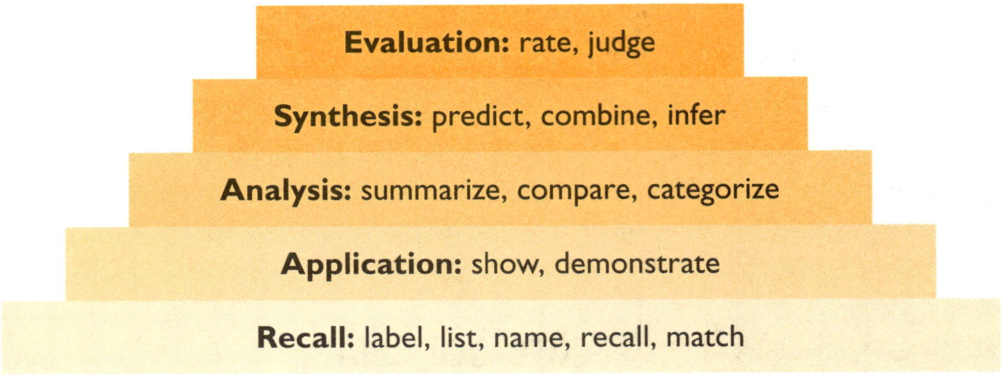

Evaluation: rate, judge
Synthesis: predict, combine, infer
Analysis: summarize, compare, categorize
Application: show, demonstrate
Recall: label, list, name, recall, match

Exercise 2.17 Identify the Hierarchy of Questions

- The popular children's book, *The Napping House* by Audrey Wood, is a delightful pattern story about a grandmother and child, along with animal friends, taking a nap on a cozy bed. The story is based on size sequence, offering a great opportunity to talk about size comparisons.
- Using this story, identify the level of the question hierarchy each question represents.

Hierarchy Level

1. Which one is bigger, the dog or the cat? _____
2. Who is on the slumbering mouse? _____
3. What is the weather like? _____
4. What happened when the flea bit the mouse? _____
5. Why did the flea bite the mouse? _____

Often, we ask children questions at the *recall* level, such as, "What (color, size, shape) is ____?" or at the *application* level, such as, "What did ____ do?" Although these elementary types of questions are important, we also need to ensure that we are asking a range of questions that will extend children's learning.

Dialogic Storybook Reading

Dialogic storybook reading is a method of shared reading in which the adult helps children become the storytellers by asking questions about the story, much like having a "dialogue" with them (Whitehurst et al., 1994; Whitehurst & Lonigan, 1998). Reading books with children is a great way to teach vocabulary, to help them expand their language, to talk about what they see, and to use more complete descriptions. Children learn more from book-reading experiences when they are actively involved.

Using this strategy, the adult is the active listener who asks questions, adding information and encouraging children to expand their descriptions and responses. Depending on the children's developmental level, their responses are expanded to more sophisticated levels and followed with more challenging questions.

General steps for dialogic reading include:
1. Always read the book yourself before you read it with children.
2. The first time you read a book with children (often in whole-group settings), you may do most of the talking. Make sure you point out things that children may not know.
3. The next time you read the same book (often in small-group settings), use general questions as a way of getting children to respond with more than one-word answers.
4. Read and talk about the book many times.

The *way* we read to children is as important as *how often* we read to them. Reading with animated expression, asking questions, and showing and discussing pictures holds children's attention. Clear routines for book reading—when it happens, who sits where, how turn-taking will be handled, etc.—need to be established. But be aware that stringent rules for participation may limit involvement and engagement (Casey & Sheran, 2004).

Build upon what children say to help them learn how to relate even longer descriptions of what they see in pictures by using language-stimulation techniques and questioning strategies. The scaffolding technique and the dialogic reading strategies as applied to book reading can also be applied to conversations with children.

Wrap-Up

Oral language is an important component of early literacy. Early childhood educators and care providers, those who have a deeper understanding of the structures of oral language and children's developmental sequences, are better able to help children develop these skills. Phonology creates the sounds for words (semantics) we say. We use word forms (morphology) and put them into sentences (syntax) and say them with expression (prosody). Language is formed from all of these structures.

The stages children go through when learning how to read are similar to those they go through when learning to talk. Children who are engaged in developmentally appropriate

Chapter 2

activities that focus on both spoken and written language tend to display improved skill and mastery in both.

When we talk to and with children, using language stimulation techniques helps build these important skills. Scaffolding techniques and dialogic storybook reading strategies are valuable ways of interacting with young children when reading books with them as well as when talking to them.

The quality of children's early experiences influences their language and literacy learning and, therefore, lifelong outcomes. We foster young children's developing language when we talk, sing, and interact with them throughout the day, during daily routines, and during play. As early childhood educators, we need to model, facilitate, and scaffold language use all day long.

Reflection and Review

1. Describe the five structures of oral language.

   _____
   _____
   _____
   _____
   _____

2. List the stages of oral language and literacy development and the characteristics of each stage.

   _____
   _____
   _____
   _____
   _____

3. Describe *language facilitation*, *scaffolding*, and *dialogic reading*, and how these techniques are used with children.
   Language facilitation: _____
   _____
   _____
   _____

Scaffolding: _____
_____
_____

Dialogic reading: _____
_____
_____
_____

4. How does knowing about the structures of oral language help us teach young children?

_____
_____
_____

Chapter 3: Phonological Awareness Connections

This chapter describes: (a) the component skills of phonological awareness; (b) a general continuum of skill development; and (c) the expected ages at which these skills should be emerging. Additionally, we will share strategies and activities that help to facilitate a range of phonological awareness skills.

Learner Objectives for Chapter 3
- Describe the component skills of phonological awareness and phonemic awareness.
- Describe the sequences of development in the areas of rhyming, alliteration, blending, and segmenting.
- Describe the linguistic hierarchy of words.
- Describe strategies that facilitate development of phonological awareness skills.

Warm-Up
- What are your thoughts about these questions? Jot down a response for each.
    1. What is your favorite nursery rhyme? What words rhyme? Are there words that begin with the same sound?
       _____
    2. What are the differences between *phonological* awareness and *phonemic* awareness?
       _____
       _____
    3. What is the *linguistic hierarchy of words*?
       _____
       _____
    4. Why, at times, is alliteration considered part of segmenting?
       _____
       _____

5. In what ways are rhyming and alliteration opposites?
   _____
   _____

6. In what ways are segmenting and blending opposites?
   _____
   _____

What Is Phonological Awareness?

Think of a time when you watched children playing with sounds in words, such as a preschool child saying, "Window, findow, mindow, bindow," or when Jason hears Josiah's name and says, "Your name sounds just like mine!" These forms of word play and focus are examples of children attending to the sound structure of words, which is the essence of phonological awareness. As one of the three foundations of early literacy, phonological awareness is a very important link between oral and written language.

Of the phonological processing abilities discussed in Chapter 1, *phonological awareness* is the most strongly related to literacy development. Remember that the definition of phonological awareness includes two important elements: the *awareness of* or *sensitivity to* speech sounds and the *ability to manipulate* the sound structures (i.e., the syllables and phonemes) in words. Phonological awareness encompasses *phoneme* or *phonemic awareness,* the understanding that words are made up of individual speech sounds and the ability to manipulate these sounds either by blending, segmenting, or changing individual sounds within words to create different words.

Exercise 3.1 — Phonological or Phonemic Awareness?

- The teacher asks, "What's this word: *e-le-phant*." The children answer, "Elephant."
  — Is this an example of phonological awareness? Phonemic awareness?

- While taking attendance, the teacher asks, "Who's here? K-K-Katy, Sh-Sh-ane … ?"
  — Is this an example of phonological awareness? Phonemic awareness?

Component Skills of Phonological Awareness

Segmenting words into syllables is a phonological awareness activity, not a phonemic awareness activity, because the focus is on parts of a word larger than a speech sound (a phoneme). Playing with the beginning sounds in children's names is phonological awareness

and phonemic awareness because you are isolating an individual sound in a word. The component skills that represent phonological awareness are:

- **Rhyming**: Match and produce word endings (rimes).
- **Alliteration**: Match and produce words with the same beginning sounds.
- **Blending**: Combine syllables and sounds to make words.
- **Segmenting**: Pull words apart into syllables and sounds.

Phonological awareness skills in kindergarten children have been identified as one of the best predictors of reading achievement between kindergarten and second grade (NRP, 2000; Snow et al., 1998; Whitehurst & Lonigan, 2002). Children who are better at playing with rhymes, syllables, and speech sounds often learn to read more quickly because these skills enable them to learn the alphabetic principle and to learn phonics. Conversely, children with underdeveloped phonological awareness skills in preschool are some of the poorest readers in later years because those students, in turn, have trouble learning how to decode.

The development of phonological awareness skills follows a general hierarchy from larger word units (syllables) to smaller ones (onset and rime units, individual speech sounds). Phonological awareness skills should begin to develop in young children well before they enter kindergarten. The word parts of oral language include:

1. Words as a whole.
2. Syllables in words: **caterpillar** = ca-ter-pil-lar .
3. Onset (initial consonant or consonant cluster of a word) and rime (the remaining vowel and consonants): In the words **cat** and **train**, the letters **c** and **tr** are the onsets, and the letters **-at** and **-ain** are the rimes.
4. Individual speech sounds in words: **cat** = /k/ /ă/ /t/.

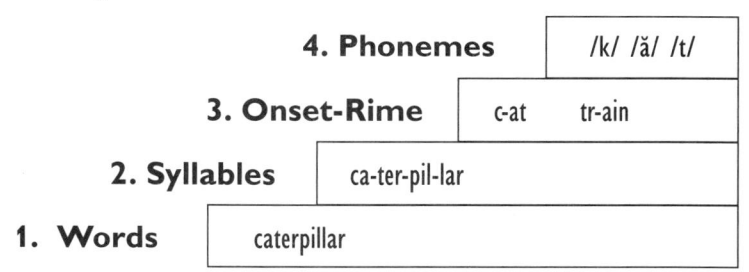

4. Phonemes	/k/ /ă/ /t/	
3. Onset-Rime	c-at	tr-ain
2. Syllables	ca-ter-pil-lar	
1. Words	caterpillar	

In the early stages of language development, children focus mainly on the meanings of the words they use and typically have little conscious awareness of the structure of the words they say. For example, when asked which word is longer, a young child may often say that the word **caterpillar** is smaller than the word **snake** because a caterpillar is smaller than a snake.

Children develop phonological awareness as they begin to realize that words have structures that are separate from the things they represent. This awareness is representative of the *metaphonological stage* of language development (discussed in Chapter 2). Children begin to realize that words are composed of syllables and sound segments (i.e., they recognize that the word **caterpillar** is longer than the word **snake**). Young children generally do better on phonological awareness tasks that involve familiar words than they do on tasks with words that are not as familiar (Metsala & Walley, 1998). Early emphasis on phonological awareness appears to put children in a better position to absorb literacy instruction later.

How Phonological Awareness Develops

During the early childhood years, many everyday routines and intentionally planned activities can be used to facilitate the development of phonological awareness skills, consisting of a wide range of word-play and sound-play interactions. Active responding is the key to teaching phonological awareness.

Teaching of phonological awareness skills has been shown to improve not only early literacy but also speech production, reading accuracy, reading comprehension, and spelling (Gillon, 2004). The ability to rhyme, identify beginning sounds, blend, segment, and in other ways manipulate the sounds in spoken words influences children's understanding of the alphabetic principle, helping them to learn that speech sounds can be represented by alphabet letters. This development is described in Chapter 4.

Rhyming

Research on developing brains has identified that when two sounds are similar (e.g., /m/ and /n/), they excite the corresponding brain cells and their neural connections. As similar sounds are heard repeatedly, the neural connections become stronger, and the sounds become more easily recognized. In this way, the brain begins to distinguish between sounds that are alike and those that are different (Wolfe & Nevills, 2004), which is essential to phonemic awareness development.

Rhyming is one of the first phonological awareness skills children display and may be the entry point for phonological awareness development (see *Table 3.1*). Rhyme knowledge at age 3 is related to success in reading and spelling at ages 5 and 6 (Bryant, MacLean, Bradley, & Crossland, 1990). Young children become sensitive to rhyme at an early age, and they are able to detect rhyme even when other phonological skills are too difficult (MacLean, Bryant, & Bradley, 1987; Whitehurst & Lonigan, 2002).

Table 3.1 Age at Which Rhyming Skills Begin to Develop

2–3 years old	Children participate in saying words in nursery rhymes, finger plays, jingles, songs, and books that are read to them.
3–5 years old	Children match words that rhyme.
4–5 years old	Children produce words that rhyme.

Exercise 3.2 | List Rhyming Words

- Think of one of your favorite fingerplays or songs for children.
- List the words that rhyme in the verses. (These language experiences help children learn how words sound similar with a focus on word structure.)

_____   _____

_____   _____

_____   _____

_____   _____

Everyday routines and strategies for early rhyming development. There are many songs, finger plays, and children's books that focus on rhyming. Here are some examples of activities that help to build a sense of rhyme:

- *Sing songs that have rhyming words.*
  For example, the "Five Little Ducks" song has several rhyming words. Pause when a rhyming word is coming and have children fill in the word (e.g., sing, "Five little ducks went out one day, over hills and far _____ "). Encourage children to fill in progressively more rhyming words in the song. Intentionally point out how some of the words sound the same at the end.

- *Read books that have rhyming words.*
  Point out how some words rhyme, or sound the same at the end. After reading the book a few times, pause to let children fill in rhyming words. For example, in the book *Is Your Mama a Llama?* by Deborah Guarine, read, "Is your mama a _____ ?" (pause to let children fill in the word). Continue, "I asked my friend Dave. 'No, she's not,' is the answer Dave _____ ." Children soon learn to fill in the words when they hear the "sameness" in how words sound.

The next skill level to develop is the ability to match words that rhyme, beginning at 3–4 years of age. Children need to actively think about the words they are considering and make a judgment about the similarity of word structure. They need to have an understanding of language at the *metaphonological* level, knowing that words have a meaning and also a structure that can be played with and manipulated.

Everyday routines and strategies for matching rhymes. Here are some examples of activities that focus on matching words that rhyme:

- *Rhyme children's names to get their attention.*
  You could say, "Jason Fason," "Molly Golly," or "Tyrone Byrone." Another idea is to say, "I need someone whose name rhymes with Tashley" when you are looking for Ashley.

- *After children have learned the verse in a nursery rhyme, change one of the rhyming words to see if the new word "works," or fits the rhyme.*
  Say, "Hickory Dickory Dock, the mouse ran up the **block**. *Dock, clock, block.* Do these words rhyme?" Then, say, "Hickory Dickory Dock, the mouse ran up the **chair**. *Dock, clock, chair.* Do these words rhyme?" Find objects for the words you use. Good words that work for the "Hickory Dickory Dock" nursery rhyme are **block**, **rock**, **sock**, and **smock**. Words that do not work can be **car**, **ball**, **horse**, etc. (Paulson et al., 2001).

The next stage to develop is producing words that rhyme, which often occurs before children enter kindergarten (Paulson, 2004). Some children have difficulty producing rhymes until they learn that words can be broken into onsets and rimes. Many times, children who struggle with learning to read have difficulty with rhyming.

Exercise 3.3   Generate Rhyming Words

- In 10 seconds, list all the words you can think of that rhyme with the word **cat**.

  _____   _____
  _____   _____
  _____   _____
  _____

  How many words did you list? _____

- In 10 seconds, list all the words you can think of that rhyme with the word **chef**.

  _____   _____
  _____   _____
  _____   _____
  _____

  How many words did you list? _____

Most likely, you were able to identify more rhyming words for **cat** than you were for **chef**. This is because the word **cat** is more common and is part of a larger word family (the -**at** pattern) than the word **chef** (the -**ef** pattern). So, when helping children learn about rhyme, choose words that they know and that have large word families. When children need more of a challenge, pick words that are not as familiar and ones with smaller word families. (Be careful with rhyming word patterns you would rather not deal with, such as **-uck** and **-itch**.)

An additional component to add to a rhyming activity is to have children identify their rhymed word as a real word or a pretend, or nonsense, word. This distinction helps children focus on word structure and word meaning, and combines phonological awareness and language development in the same activity. For example, when saying a rhyming word for **bug**, pre-kindergartener Carrie says, "*Bug, rug.* A **rug** is for the floor. *Bug, wug.* I don't know what a **wug** is." She has to process whether or not she understands that word, deepening her understanding of how words work.

Everyday routines and strategies for producing rhymes. Here are some examples of activities that focus on producing words that rhyme:

- *Change the beginning sound in words for things you refer to, such as food items you provide for snacks or when you give directions.*
  You might say, "We are having *mocolate mudding*" instead of **chocolate pudding**. When getting ready to go outside, you could say, "It's time to put on your *poats* and *dittens* to go *routside*." Have children identify a real word that rhymes with your silly word. A good book to read that promotes this activity is *The Hungry Thing* by Jan Slepian and Ann Seidler. In this book, a creature comes to town and wants to eat "smankakes" and "sickles," but he really wants *pancakes* and *pickles*. Children love it, and the concept of changing words in their environment is engaging and effective in helping them learn about rhyming (Paulson et al., 2001).
- *Read the story* There's a Wocket in My Pocket *by Dr. Seuss.*
  Have children invent their own characters, draw pictures of their characters with the rhyming object, then write (or narrate) a sentence that describes where their character is (e.g., "There's a *zarpet* on my *carpet*"). Create a classroom book with the children's illustrations of rhyming characters (Paulson et al., 2001).
- *Read the book* Sam's Sandwich *by David Pelham.*
  This is an engaging (and somewhat gross) flap book that has pictures of bugs hiding under the page flaps of the sandwich ingredients. Have children identify the rhyme. Make your own pages with two starter sentences written on a page and a folded flap at the bottom of the page. Have children think of two things that would be gross to eat that also rhyme with the real words. Have them draw a picture of each item and complete the starter sentences with words that rhyme. They can write or narrate their words to you (Paulson et al., 2001).
  "Inside my sandwich was a ... (snake)."
  "Looking further, I found a... (rake)."
  "Inside my sandwich was a ... (pig)."
  "Looking further, I found a... (wig)."

For more rhyming activities, see *Building Early Literacy and Language Skills* (Paulson et al., 2001).

Alliteration

Alliteration is the identification and production of words that begin with the same initial sound. As children are exposed to words and the sounds in words, they learn to focus on the beginnings of words (sound detection) and categorize words by their initial sound (sound categorization) (Gillon, 2004; Moats, 2009). Because alliteration requires sensitivity to word parts that are smaller than a syllable at the sound level, this is a beginning phonemic awareness skill. The ability to focus on beginning sounds of words is an early step in sound, or phoneme, segmentation. Children with good alliteration skills are often good readers (Bryant et al., 1990) because phoneme awareness underlies the ability to match sounds with symbols.

The developmental sequence of alliteration is similar to that of rhyming; however, alliteration does not develop as early in the preschool years as rhyme (see *Table 3.2*). Children first learn to identify and match words that begin with the same sounds, then they learn to produce words that begin with a given sound. Four-year-olds begin to notice and match words that have the same beginning sound and identify which word begins with a given sound. This skill is often established by the time children are 5 years old (Paulson, 2004).

Table 3.2 Age at Which Alliteration Skills Begin to Develop

3–5 years old	Children recognize words with a common initial sound.
5–7 years old	Children produce words with a common initial sound.

Sometimes, identifying the beginning sound of words can be a challenge for us literate adults if we focus on the way a word is *written* instead of how a word is *said*. What sound does the word **cow** begin with? If you said /k/, you are right. If you said a "**c**" sound, you are referring to the *letter* that the word **cow** starts with, not the *sound*.

Exercise 3.4 Isolate Initial Sounds

- Identify the beginning sound of each word (e.g., /b/, /d/).

sun ____	write ____	fish ____	cup ____	zipper ____
sugar ____	white ____	phone ____	cent ____	xylophone ____
shoe ____	ring ____	pole ____	chair ____	
			Chris ____	

Everyday routines and strategies for alliteration. There are many ways to focus on the beginning sounds of words in everyday routines and activities. Remember that alliteration is also similar to segmenting initial sounds in words. Here are some examples:

Recognition
- Read books with words that begin with the same sound. Point out these words to children, and demonstrate how to say the sounds. A couple of good books that stress alliteration are *Silly Sally* by Audrey Wood and *Leo the Late Bloomer* by Robert Kraus.
- Play with children's names, and point out things that begin with the same beginning sound as their names.
- Identify children's names or the names of objects by saying the first sound (onset) and then the rest of the name (rime) (e.g., say, "I see **S-am**" or " I see a **b-all**"). This activity highlights the sound structures in words and how words work.
- Play with words by "bouncing" on the beginnings sounds of children's names or the names of other objects (e.g., say, "I see **J-J-J-Jenna**" or say "I see a **d-d-d-dog**") (Paulson et al., 2001).

Matching
- In a guessing game, say, "I'm thinking of something (or someone) that starts with … (say a speech sound)." Or, "I need someone whose name starts with …. (say a speech sound)."

Production
- While showing children an animal puppet, tell them that this puppet likes to eat only things that begin with the same sound as the kind of animal he or she is. Have children identify the kind of animal and then the foods that the puppet eats (e.g., a **m**onkey puppet would like to eat only **m**uffins, **m**eatloaf, **m**ilk, **m**ashed potatoes, etc.; a **p**enguin puppet would like to eat only **p**opcorn, **p**ickles, **p**udding, **p**izza, etc.).

Note: In a sense, rhyming and alliteration are opposite skills, with rhyme focusing on the end of words and alliteration focusing on the beginning of words. Young children are often able to participate in rhyme and alliteration activities but may be confused when these activities are done consecutively and by the words you have them manipulate. For example: You present one preschool activity that focuses on words beginning with the same sound, using the words **bus** and **book**. Then, you immediately follow with an activity that focuses on rhyme matching, using pictures to match the words **bus**, **book**, and **hook**. When you ask children to choose the two words that rhyme, they may respond with **bus** and **book**, because they are still focusing on the beginning sound, not the rhyme. It is very important to give clear directions and distinct descriptions for each of these separate activities and to provide many word examples as young children learn what we mean when we rhyme or focus on beginning sounds.

Blending

Blending is the ability to combine a sequence of isolated syllables or sounds together to produce a recognizable word. Blending words from syllables is an early developing phonological awareness skill and an easy one to teach. Blending sounds reflects the abstract nature of reading (Moats, 2009) and is related to a child's later ability to decode printed words (Catts, 1991). Once again, the blending skills of young children entering school are highly predictive of how well they will learn to read.

The development of blending (see *Table 3.3*) follows the linguistic hierarchy of larger to smaller units of speech—from words to syllables to onset-rimes to individual speech sounds (Adams, 1990; Anthony, Lonigan, Burgess, Driscoll, Phillips, et al., 2002). Generally, 3- and 4-year-old children learn to blend syllables into words and progress to sound units. Children entering kindergarten should be able to blend sounds into words.

Table 3.3 Age at Which Blending Skills Begin to Develop

3–4 years old	Children combine a sequence of isolated *syllables* to produce words.
4–5 years old	Children combine a sequence of isolated *sounds* to produce words.

Exercise 3.5 Determine the Level of Linguistic Analysis

- What is the linguistic level of each example: *syllable*, *onset-rime*, or *phoneme*?

    1. A teacher says, "I see a **kan-ga-roo**!" and children reply, "Kangaroo!"
    _____

    2. A teacher says, "I want to see **T-asha**," and Tasha comes over.
    _____

    3. A teacher says, "I want a block that is **r-e-d**," and a child provides a red block.
    _____

Segmenting

Segmenting, the opposite skill of blending, requires the ability to analyze the components of a word and pull them apart (segment) into syllables, onsets and rimes, or individual speech sounds. Phoneme, or sound, segmentation is a skill that is related to success in beginning reading and is also an important step to learning letter-sound correspondences (Catts, 1991; Moats, 2009; National Institute of Child Health and Human Development [NICHD], 2000).

Like blending, the development of segmenting follows the same hierarchy, from larger to smaller word units. However, for young children, segmenting words at the phoneme level is

Phonological Awareness Connections

typically harder than blending phonemes. Three and 4-year-olds learn to segment syllables into words and then progress to sound units (see *Table 3.4*). By the time children enter kindergarten, they should be able to segment the beginning sound (onset) from the rest of a word (rime); then, they should learn to isolate individual sounds of simple words with consonant-vowel-consonant (CVC) patterns, such as **fig**, **sun**, and **hat**.

Table 3.4 Age at Which Segmenting Skills Begin to Develop

3–4 years old	Children identify *syllables* in words.
4–5 years old	Children identify *beginning sounds* in words.
5–6 years old	Children identify *sounds* in one-syllable words.

Some programs designed to teach phonological awareness begin with teaching children to segment words in sentences. According to Gillon (2004), there is little evidence to support a connection between this level of awareness and word recognition or spelling ability. Certainly, understanding the concept of a word is important as an oral language skill. When working on building phonological awareness, a focus on segmenting sentences into words before segmenting syllables in words may not be necessary.

Exercise 3.6 Identify Syllables and Phonemes

- List ten different kinds of animals, and identify the number of syllables in each name.

  1. _____   _____
  2. _____   _____
  3. _____   _____
  4. _____   _____
  5. _____   _____
  6. _____   _____
  7. _____   _____
  8. _____   _____
  9. _____   _____
  10. _____   _____

(continued)

Exercise 3.6 (continued)

- List ten animal pairs whose names begin with the same sound (e.g., **d**og, **d**onkey; **c**at, **c**amel).

    1. _____
    2. _____
    3. _____
    4. _____
    5. _____
    6. _____
    7. _____
    8. _____
    9. _____
    10. _____

- List five animal names that have only one syllable, and identify the sounds and number of sounds in each name.

    1. _____ _____
    2. _____ _____
    3. _____ _____
    4. _____ _____
    5. _____ _____

Everyday routines and strategies for blending and segmenting. Just as rhyming and alliteration skills are opposites, in a sense, so are the skills of blending and segmenting. However, unlike rhyming and alliteration, blending and segmenting activities go hand in hand. There are many ways to embed blending and segmenting into everyday routines and activities. Here are some examples following the linguistic hierarchy:

Phonological Awareness Connections

Syllables
- In opening Circle time, have children segment and blend each other's names to the tune of the song "Hickety Pickety Bumble Bee, can you say your name for me?" (Using a bee puppet while children sing is a nice visual addition.) Have each child take a turn saying his or her name, then have all children say that child's name in a segmented manner, clapping their hands on their knees for each syllable (Paulson et al., 2001).
- In a calendar routine talking about the day, have children segment and blend the name of the month, the day, the type of weather outside, etc. (e.g., **Jan-u-ar-y, Tues-day, sun-ny**).
- When reading books to children, talk about the pictures and say the names of the picture objects in a segmented manner. (The book *Polar Bear, Polar Bear, What Do You Hear?* by Bill Martin, Jr. works well for this activity.) Segment the name of the animal on the page for children to blend and identify, either by the syllables or the beginning sound.
- Use "Robot Reporting" (Paulson et al., 2001) when giving children directions by talking like a robot, segmenting the words in your directions (e.g., **"We – are – go-ing – to – the – li-bra-ry – to-day"**).

Syllables, Onset-Rimes, Phonemes
- When you ask children for an item, say the word in a segmented manner and have them find what you are asking for by blending the word (e.g., *syllables*: **"I need the news-pa-per"**; *onset-rime*: **"I need a b-ook"**; *phonemes*: **"I need a /k/ /ō/ /t/"**). Have children segment the names of items at their linguistic level.
- Talk about food items you are providing for a meal or a snack. Say the names of the foods in a segmented manner, then have children blend the words (e.g., **"Today we are having straw-ber-ries"**). Have children segment the names of food items at their linguistic level.
- Play "I Spy," looking for items around the environment. For example, say to children, "I see an **a-quar-i-um**," then ask them to blend the syllables and respond with **aquarium**. Have children play "I Spy" as they find an item, then segment the word into syllables or sounds.
- Collect a variety of small objects and put them in an opaque bag (so that the items cannot be seen) for a "Grab Bag Surprise" (Paulson et al., 2001). Choose an object and hide it in your hand. Say the name of the item in a segmented manner so that children can blend the word to guess what is in your hand. Have children participate by choosing an item and segmenting the name for their friends to blend.
- Find pictures of items that are part of a thematic unit you may be focusing on in your setting. (Get pictures from magazines, clip art, old pictures that are not used for other purposes, etc.) Cut the pictures into "picture puzzles" for children to put together and take apart (blend and segment) (Paulson et al., 2001; see *Figure 3.1*, next page).

- For example, if you are focusing on a transportation unit, cut out pictures of a motorcycle, bicycle, helicopter, taxi, and canoe into the number of pieces for *each syllable* in the word (i.e., cut the picture of the motorcycle into four pieces, the bicycle into three pieces, the taxi into two pieces, etc.).
- With another set of pictures, cut them into picture puzzles that represent the word's *onset* (first sound) and *rime* (the rest of the word) (i.e., two-piece picture puzzles for **c-ar**, **b-oat**, **j-eep**, **b-us**, **b-ike**, etc.).
- Finally, make another set of picture puzzles of one-syllable words that are cut into the number of pieces that represents the *number of sounds* in the word (i.e., a two-piece picture puzzle for **c-ar** [/k/ /ar/]; three-piece picture puzzles for **b-oa-t** [/b/ /ō/ /t/], **b-u-s** [/b/ /ŭ/ /s/], **j-ee-p** [/j/ /ē/ /p/], **b-i-ke** [/b/ /ī/ /k/], etc.).

Figure 3.1 Picture Puzzle Formats for Blending and Segmenting

Syllables — BI | CY | CLE (bicycle)

Syllables — MO | TOR | CY | CLE (motorcycle)

Onset-Rime — C | AR (car)

Phonemes — B | OA | T (boat)

Remember: Syllables are easier than beginning sounds, and individual sounds are the most difficult for young children to distinguish.

Hierarchy of Phonological Awareness Skill Development

Paulson (2004) conducted a study to investigate the levels of skill acquisition and to compare the relative difficulty among phonological awareness tasks in 80 typically developing, pre-kindergarten 4- and 5-year-old children. A collection of ten tasks in a range of linguistic complexity was used to measure phonological awareness subskills in the areas of rhyming, alliteration, blending, and segmenting (see *Table 3.5*). Rhyming tasks included detection and production. Alliteration tasks included detection and sound categorization. Blending and segmenting each included tasks of syllables, onset-rime units, and phonemes.

Table 3.5 Phonological Awareness Skills in Developmental Order
(Paulson, 2004)

Rhyming	• matching • production
Alliteration	• matching • categorization
Blending	• syllables • onset-rime units • phonemes
Segmenting	• syllables • onset-rime units • phonemes

The results indicated a significant difference between the age groups in six-month increments in each of the phonological awareness component skills. A general hierarchy of skill acquisition was identified for the group as a whole and for each age group, describing which skills were easiest through the most difficult. The results suggest a developmental continuum of phonological awareness skills leading to phonemic awareness in young children before entering kindergarten. Identification of this skill acquisition and hierarchy is an important consideration in planning appropriate and effective early childhood instruction and to monitor children's progress in developing their understanding of the sound structure of language.

Children in this study were easily able to blend and segment syllables and match words that rhyme; the most difficult tasks were those that involved individual phonemes. *Table 3.6* (next page) identifies the skills that were the easiest to the most difficult for both age groups. Before entering kindergarten, these young children certainly were developing phonological awareness skills, but they had *not* yet developed competent levels of phonemic awareness (Paulson, 2004).

Table 3.6 Ranking of Percent Correct Scores of
Phonological Awareness Skills for 4- and 5-Year-Old Children
(Paulson, 2004)

Rank	4-Year-Olds	Percentage	5-Year-Olds	Percentage
1	Blending syllables	84	Blending syllables	92
2	Segmenting syllables	62	Rhyme detection	81
3	Rhyme detection	58	Alliteration categorization	74
4	Alliteration categorization	53	Segmenting syllables	71
5	Blending onset-rime units	42	Rhyme production	61
6	Alliteration detection	32	Blending onset-rime units	57
7	Rhyme production	31	Alliteration detection	54
8	Blending phonemes	13	Blending phonemes	29
9	Segmenting onset-rime	8	Segmenting onset-rime	22
10	Segmenting phonemes	3	Segmenting phonemes	7
Both Groups Combined				
1	Blending syllables	88%		
2	Rhyme detection	70%		
3	Segmenting syllables	67%		
4	Alliteration categorization	63%		
5	Blending onset-rime units	49%		
6	Rhyme production	47%		
7	Alliteration detection	43%		
8	Blending phonemes	21%		
9	Segmenting onset-rime	15%		
10	Segmenting phonemes	5%		

Wrap-Up

Phonological awareness is an important aspect of early literacy that is related to reading success later in school and is an important link between oral and written language. Component skills include rhyming, alliteration, blending, and segmenting within a linguistic hierarchy of speech structures such as syllables, onset-rime units, and phonemes (sounds).

Phonological awareness skills typically begin to develop in young children well before they enter kindergarten. There are many opportunities to include phonological awareness instruction into everyday routines and activities in playful and developmentally appropriate ways at school and at home. Just as with other skills, children typically display a range of phonological awareness skill development. For many children—especially those with language delays or who are at risk of having learning disabilities—specific instruction is required to help them develop an understanding of the structures of speech sounds and words, which in turn is necessary to understand how speech is represented in written form. Developing appropriate training of phonological awareness skills in young children puts them on the right road to reading.

Reflection and Review

1. What are the four components of phonological awareness?

2. List the developmental sequences of each component of phonological awareness.

3. What strategies can be used to build phonological awareness in young children?

Chapter 4: Written Language Connections

This chapter describes the development of print knowledge, the third foundation of early literacy. Print knowledge encompasses three components: (a) an awareness of the concepts of print; (b) an understanding of the written symbols that represent spoken language; and (c) learning to be a writer. We will describe what young children do and how we can help them in these three areas.

Learner Objectives for Chapter 4
- Describe print awareness concepts and at what ages young children generally learn them.
- Describe how and at what ages young children learn about letter knowledge and the alphabetic principle.
- Describe the importance of having young children learn about the writing process.

Warm-Up
- What are your thoughts about these questions? Jot down a response for each.
  1. List a few examples of print concepts that young children should learn.

     _____

     _____

  2. How many letters do young children typically know before they enter kindergarten?

     _____

     _____

  3. What is the *alphabetic principle,* and why is it important in the literacy learning process?

     _____

     _____

4. Which are easier for young children to recognize and write: uppercase or lowercase letters?
   _____
   _____

5. How do the stages of writing development match up with the stages of literacy development?
   _____
   _____

Concepts of Print

Print is everywhere in our lives, surrounding us with alphabetic symbols that are part of our world. Words are on the clothes we wear, the signs we see, the bags we carry, the books we read, and the toys we play with. Long before children learn to read and write, they begin to understand how alphabetic symbols work. Children need visual and physical interactions with print to learn print concepts, alphabet knowledge, and how to write. Multiple exposures to print in the early years help to build the foundation children need for literacy acquisition and motivation for learning to read and write.

A central literacy goal during the preschool and kindergarten years is teaching print awareness concepts, such as recognizing environmental print and learning how print works (Bredekamp, & Copple, 1998). In children's everyday routines, opportunities abound in exposing them to the symbols, logos, and graphics that represent the written language system. Helping young children to see print, learn what print is used for, and see how print is made helps them develop an understanding of the concepts of print. When children's experiences to print are limited, they lack the exposure needed to figure out how print works and puts them at risk for having problems learning to read and write.

> **Print awareness concepts include:**
> - recognizing print in the environment;
> - understanding that print carries meaning;
> - knowing that print is used for many purposes; and
> - experiencing print through writing.

Print awareness concepts that are important for young children to be exposed to include:

1. **Recognizing print in their surroundings.**
   Children learn to recognize written symbols in their environment, such as the logo of their favorite fast-food restaurant or the red octagon on the street corner that says "Stop." Their beginning understanding is a *visual* recognition based on how the symbol or word looks (i.e., the prealphabetic, or logographic, level of literacy development).

2. **Understanding that print carries meaning.**
   As children participate in book-reading with adult guidance and instruction:

- They recognize pictures on a page and know that those images represent the "real thing."
- They learn that the print, or the "black, squiggly lines," are the words that tell the story.
- They learn that you start reading at the top of a page, then continue to the bottom.
- They learn to sweep their index finger across the words, moving from left to right.
- When a familiar book is read to them, they subsequently learn to point to each word individually.
- They learn to recognize book features, such as the front and back covers, the title, etc.
- They learn that books are written by authors and have drawings made by illustrators.
- And, importantly, they learn how to handle books appropriately.

3. **Knowing that print is used for many purposes.**
   With multiple, varied, and different exposures, children learn that:
   - Print is in books, magazines, and newspapers.
   - Print is on storefronts, cereal boxes, and other containers.
   - You use print when making cookies or pudding by following recipes.
   - You use print to make a list of things you need at the grocery store or of chores you need to do.
   - Birthday cards, notes, and mail have print.
   - Print is on computers, TV shows, and video games.
   - Many toys and tangible learning tools—including puzzles, blocks, magnetic letters, and electronic educational toys—highlight alphabet letters and numerals.

4. **Experiencing print through writing.**
   When young children see others pick up a pen or pencil and write, they want to do the same. They want to make what they recognize as squiggly marks on paper or, sometimes, any available surface.

All of these types and mediums of exposure help build children's understanding of the concepts of print and how print works.

How Children Develop Print Awareness

Learning to make sense of print begins with caring adults who provide children with a positive climate for developing an interest in print and a love of books. Children's language skills expand because of what they learn from having books read to, and with, them. Typically, with rich exposure to print, children progress through a developmental continuum as they begin to learn the skills related to print development.

Babies and Toddlers

Infants love to listen to the sound of the human voice, so they can be read to from birth. As they begin to actively manipulate items in their world, they will experiment with board and cloth books by banging, dropping, and chewing on them. When adults point to and talk about the pictures, babies will begin to want to look at the pictures too, for very short periods of time.

With these introductory experiences, children learn to recognize covers of specific books. They learn that books are handled in particular ways, they hold their favorite books right side up, and they learn to turn the pages. Toddlers look at pictures and label objects in books, and they realize that pictures are symbols for real objects. They want to share book-reading routines with their primary caregivers and will request favorite books. They also may begin to recognize some shapes, symbols, signs, and letters in their environment; logos for stores and restaurants they have been to; containers they recognize; and their favorite toys.

3- to 4-Year-Olds

With adult support, preschoolers extend their understanding of written language as they learn that the letters of the alphabet are a special category of visual graphics that can be individually named. They recognize many signs and logos in their environment. They know that print is read in stories and understand that print has different functions (e.g., lists for groceries, logos for favorite places and things, longer lines of print in books). They show a greater interest in books and display reading and writing attempts. They may look for the first letter of their name in print.

4- to 5-Year-Olds

Older preschool children learn that writing is used to convey messages and that it has a specific form and symbol structure. They recognize and read some words in the environment and also recognize, name, and write many alphabet letters. They are developing an understanding of the alphabetic principle (i.e., an understanding that letters represent speech sounds), may try to sound out and write simple words, and will want to write and dictate stories.

Ways to Help Young Children Develop Print Awareness

Print is an integral part of our daily routines. As adults, we often do not pay much attention to the print around us or the routine features of books and book handling. We just know that, in English, we begin at the top of the page and move to the bottom, and read words from left to right. We know that words are separated by spaces and that sentences begin with capital letters and end with some kind of punctuation mark. These are all important concepts to intentionally teach young children when we are reading books to them and talking with them about print.

Print Awareness for Babies

- Choose books that are visually interesting, that stand up, and that have large, simple pictures or designs set against a contrasting background.
- Select cloth and vinyl books that are easy for babies to pick up and do not disintegrate when wet, being cleaned, or chewed on.
- Point to pictures for the pleasure of the sights and sounds on the pages. (It is often more enjoyable for babies to handle books than to "read" them.)
- Point out objects, pictures, and words in the baby's environment.
- Expose babies to writing and reading that occur in their environment.

Print Awareness for Toddlers

- Read toddlers' favorite books over and over.
- Select books that have familiar pictures (e.g., young children and adults in everyday roles, animals, familiar objects and events, favorite TV characters) and include well-known songs.
- Point to words on a page with your index finger while reading top to bottom and left to right.
- Talk about events in books that can be related to everyday routines and the environment.

Print Awareness for 3- to 4-Year-Olds

- Provide children with a wide variety of reading material and objects (e.g., books, catalogs, photo albums, magazines, calendars, keyboards, calculators).
- Provide many playful experiences with print, both reading and writing.
- Add books to read multiple times.
- Keep reading old favorites.
- Point out the titles of books.
- Occasionally, point to specific words as you read them.
- When you finish reading a page, ask the child what to read next.
- Point out print, symbols, and words in the environment.
- Demonstrate how print is used in everyday routines (e.g., cooking, going shopping, finding something in a catalog, checking the calendar, making signs).

Print Awareness for 4- to 5-Year-Olds

- Continue to involve children in playful experiences with print.
- Help children make signs, write their own stories, and dictate stories to go along with their play.
- Write down children's spoken stories and create books about them.
- Continue to read to, and with, children, sharing their favorite books and new ones.
- Encourage children to tell stories with increasingly complex plots and events.

Concepts of print are just one aspect of young children's early literacy development. Young children also need developmentally appropriate experiences and guided, intentional teaching to support their literacy learning in print-rich environments.

We need to intentionally draw children's attention to the symbols in the environment; point out specific letters and words; read high-quality books on a daily basis with individual children and in small groups; use books that positively reflect children's identity, home language, and culture; and provide many opportunities to engage in play that incorporates literacy tools (e.g., writing grocery lists in dramatic play, making street signs when building a town with blocks, using icons and words in exploring a computer game). With our help, preschoolers learn to recognize print, know its meaning, understand its purpose, and figure out how it is written.

Exercise 4.1 Inform Instruction About Print Concepts

- List three ways you can help children develop their concepts of print in each of these areas:

  1. Recognizing print in our surroundings:
     - _____
     - _____
     - _____

  2. Understanding that print carries meaning:
     - _____
     - _____
     - _____

  3. Knowing that print is used for many purposes:
     - _____
     - _____
     - _____

  4. Experiencing print through writing:
     - _____
     - _____
     - _____

Alphabet Knowledge That Leads to the Alphabetic Principle

Some early childhood educators have questioned teaching preschool children directly about letters. Is the alphabet, a collection of abstract symbols, truly meaningful to preschoolers?

Research has shown that many children who are successful in learning to read knew letter names and developed an understanding of sound connections to letters during the preschool years (Snow, Burns, & Griffin, 1998). We do not expect preschoolers to know all the letters of the alphabet, but many toddlers (Burgess, 2006) and preschool children know letters that are important to them, such as the letters in their names (Neuman et al., 2000). They also learn that the alphabet plays a unique role in our lives, helping us to communicate. As they learn about the letters of the alphabet, young children learn how the letters represent the sounds in the words they are reading and writing and transition from the logographic to the *early alphabetic stage* of literacy development.

The idea that individual sounds in spoken words are represented by written symbols is the underpinning of alphabetic knowledge. The ability to identify letter names is known to be one of the most powerful predictors of early reading ability (NICHD, 2000) and has consequently become a standard early literacy measure in preschool and kindergarten.

Alphabetic knowledge leads to the development of the *alphabetic principle*, the understanding that there is a systematic relationship between speech sounds and letters (Adams, 2002) (see *Figure 4.1*). Because letters and words are the building blocks of print, understanding the alphabetic principle is necessary for early reading. Children need to learn how the sounds of their oral language relate to print. In order to do this, children must have some sensitivity to speech sounds or a basic level of phonemic awareness (Ashby & Rayner, 2006).

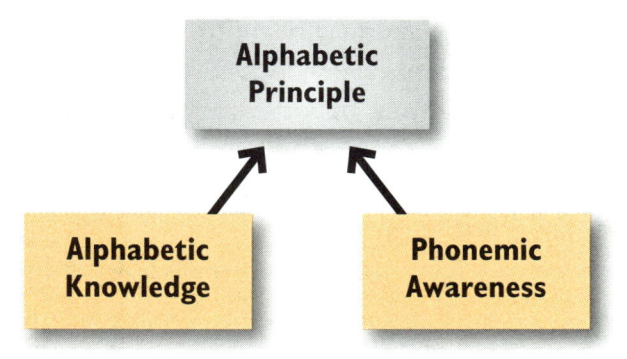

Figure 4.1 Foundations of the Alphabetic Principle

Alphabetic Principle ← **Alphabetic Knowledge** + **Phonemic Awareness**

How Young Children Synthesize Letters and Words

Children who live in a literate environment begin to figure out that there are relationships between oral and written language. When adults expose children to reading and writing, their natural curiosity leads them to form ideas about print and its use in their lives. When learning alphabet letter names, young children typically follow the sequence as listed in *Table 4.1* (next page).

Table 4.1 The Learning Sequence of Letters and Words

Skill Behavior	Age Range
Recognize and name a few letters.	2–3 years
Recognize beginning letters in familiar words.	3–4 years
Learn both uppercase and lowercase letters.	3–5 years
Relate some letters to specific sounds that the letters represent.	4–6 years

Preschool accomplishments of 3- to 4- year-olds include knowledge that the letters of the alphabet are a special category of visual symbols that can be individually named. Preschoolers can identify an average of ten alphabet letters, especially those in their names (Shaywitz, 2003; Snow et al., 1998). Four- to 5-year-old preschoolers can recognize and name a growing number of letters; and children entering kindergarten often recognize and name almost all uppercase and lowercase letters.

By the end of kindergarten, children should readily recognize and name all the letters of the alphabet (both uppercase and lowercase) and be able to identify the speech sounds that the letters represent. To enable them to do so, we give them ample experiences with letters throughout the preschool and kindergarten years. Yet in all classrooms, a range of skill development will exist. If children have not had experiences with or exposure to letter names or if they have difficulty learning these skills, we need to teach them directly.

Ways to Help Young Children Learn Their ABCs (and DEFs)

The alphabet and printed words constitute the foundation of a literate life. Long before they go to school, young children may learn to spot letters that are important to them (e.g., the beginning letter of their name) and may begin to notice the general shape and length of a few familiar words. As educators, our job is to create print-rich environments and to intentionally provide many learning opportunities for young children. The National Association for the Education of Young Children (NAEYC) (Neuman et al., 2000) recommends these teaching aids for alphabet-letter exposure, as well as their placement, in a developmentally appropriate, print-rich environment:

- Place alphabet displays at children's eye level—not above their heads—so that they can easily examine the displays.
- Print the alphabet in sets of uppercase and lowercase letters that correspond to the phrases in the "ABC" song (i.e., ABCD on the first line, EFG on the second line, etc.), as in *Figure 4.2*.

Figure 4.2 ABC/abc Eye Chart
(from *BELLS*, Paulson et al., 2001)

ABC Eye Chart
A B C D
E F G
H I J K
L M N O P
Q R S
T U V
W X
Y Z

abc Eye Chart
a b c d
e f g
h i j k
l m n o p
q r s
t u v
w x
y z

- Place letter strips where children can easily find them as they work and play:
  — Put alphabet strips on worktables.
  — Laminate letter-writing guides, and place them on a shelf or a peg. Children can help themselves to the guides and take them along to wherever they are writing.
- Have letter shapes in different media forms—alphabet puzzles, letter-shaped cookie cutters for pushing in to damp sand or play dough, magnetic letters, alphabet blocks —available for children to handle. These different types of materials allow children to explore letter-sound connections, arrange and rearrange letters, and become more aware of the sequence of sounds and letter patterns within the alphabet sequence and in words.

Children need to recognize both uppercase and lowercase forms of letters. Although recognizing the latter form is crucial for reading text, uppercase letters are more easily distinguished from each other. Adams (1990) recommends that when working with preschool children, begin with teaching uppercase letters, then lowercase letters. It is not necessary to wait until children have learned all uppercase letters before introducing lowercase forms. There are 40 distinctive letters for children to learn when the 12 uppercase-lowercase mates are considered (Ehri & Roberts, 2006). Letter names should be taught before letter sounds (Adams, 1990; Ehri & Roberts, 2006).

We should call this a 'wubble-woo' instead of a 'double you.'

Here are a few suggestions for helping children learn the letters of the alphabet and how letters group together to make words:

- As you plan your daily routines, make sure that children have many opportunities to identify letters, to write letters, and to find out how letters function to represent sounds in words.
- Put children's names on cubbies, attendance chart, job charts, etc. Draw attention to the first letters in their names (e.g., "I see we have three children whose names start with **T**"). Or use the first letters in children's names for transitions (e.g., "If your name starts with **M**, you can line up"). At first, show everyone a large printed target letter or point to it on an alphabet chart. Then, introduce letter sounds (e.g., "If your name begins with /m/, like **Max**, you can line up").
- Using their repertoire of known letters and cues (e.g., word length), encourage children to figure out the meanings of the print they see on signs, their T-shirts, and in greeting cards, magazines, or books. You might ask, "Can anyone tell me which of the words on our shopping list is **juice**? " Or, "Jason isn't here today. Can you please find his placemat for me, Jenny?"
- Have a variety of crafts materials—yarn, pipe cleaners, foam shapes, play dough—available for children to make letters out of.
- Create a Writing Center where children can experiment with different writing tools (e.g., pens, pencils, crayons, markers, chalk, stamps, stencils).
- Have a collection of alphabet books to look at and read aloud.
- Give children plastic alphabet tiles and encourage them to spell their names and other words they know and like.
- Have children guess the letter you are writing as you draw parts of it, one part at a time.
- Play matching and memory games with individual letters written on cards.
- Post the alphabet song in your classroom, and sing it every day. (A great time is when children are washing their hands before and after eating a snack or while they are standing in a line.)

Exercise 4.2 — Make Letter Forms

- Cut the shapes below out of sturdy material, such as thin foam, thin wood, or cardboard. (This activity has been around for a long time and is now a component in the *Handwriting Without Tears*® series by Jan Olsen [1998]).
- Use these shapes to create letters of the alphabet. To make one set of all uppercase and lowercase letters, you will need:
  — two large stick shapes;
  — two large half-circles;
  — three small stick shapes;
  — three small half-circles; and
  — one small circle.

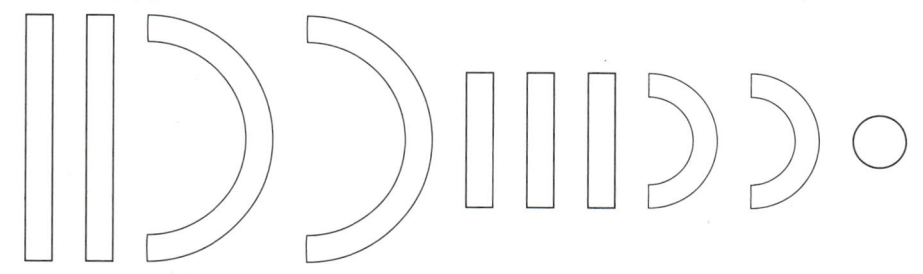

- By creating multiple sets for your classroom, you and your children can make letters and words with these pieces. Or, as an extension activity, have children play with these pieces to create other shapes and objects.

Becoming a Writer: From Scribbles to Letters

Young children learn about the concepts of print and how print works not only through reading but also through writing. When they see others pick up a pen or pencil and write, they want to do the same. They want to make what they recognize as squiggly marks on paper, or on any surface that is available. Much of their "writing" is a kind of exploratory play. Writing experiences for young children are appropriate and successful when they are fun as well as meaningful.

In this section, we will look at why writing is important during the early childhood years, how writing develops, and how we can help young children become writers.

Why Writing Is Important

Writing is a complex process that requires the integration of a number of skills and develops in a sequence of identified stages. These skills include an understanding of print, the development of motor skills, and the generation of ideas. Skills that need to be taught to young children throughout the development of writing include pencil grip, letter formation, letter-sound correspondences, and conventions of print.

In the early stages of writing drawing, adults should encourage the exploration of writing materials and letter-sound relationships, and all writing attempts also should be encouraged. In later stages, the focus will shift to penmanship, spelling, and composition development.

The ability to write has not always been considered an important component of the early childhood curriculum. A common strategy—which is still recommended—has been to write children's stories for them. Young children also should be encouraged to use "kid" writing, or temporary writing. This seminal form suggests that we know their writing is not grown-up or conventional, but it is, indeed, the kind of writing young children create. When they are encouraged to produce their own "writing," young children feel comfortable taking risks and exploring their sense of written language.

One of the identified ways that preschool programs make a difference in young children's literacy development is to provide them with many opportunities to write, guided by adults in small-group time (Dickinson & Tabors, 2001). Studies have shown that preschool children who have had regular opportunities to express themselves on paper, without feeling too constrained for correct spelling and proper handwriting, have a better understanding that writing has real purpose (Sulzby, 1985). Within this strategy, our job is to guide young children through the writing stages, allowing them to participate in the act of problem solving to identify the letter(s) that represent sounds in the words they are writing as well as helping them to develop appropriate pencil grip and letter formation. A focus on correct spelling and handwriting is part of the process; when these skills are taught within an educational curriculum, they should be expected.

Encouraging writing during the preschool years, modeling the stages of print, and praising children's attempts to write have become standard practices in early childhood settings. By setting up a Writing Center and a writing program, we can encourage developmental and functional writing. Through early attempts at drawing and writing—whatever level that may be—children will have a first-hand opportunity to learn about print and writing.

Young children often write using big letters and making a lot of line overruns (Schickedanz & Casbergue, 2004). They may hold the writing tool with a tight fist grip and press down hard enough to tear paper. Difficulty in forming letters is not related to cognitive skills but to fine-motor development. Movements using a rigid fist grip come from the muscle of the upper arm, not smaller hand movements. As a result, these rigid movements make it difficult for children to shape letters with precision. In activities that help develop small-muscle control, children learn to relax their arm muscles and form the lines, circles, and scribbles that start to resemble writing (Machado, 1999).

The Five Stages of Writing Development

Children's writing develops in a well-defined sequence that represents their understanding of how print works. As children play with writing, they move from imitating patterns to creating them. They begin to attend to specific print, such as the letters in their names, and will write messages they expect adults to read. The stages begin with simple scribbles and progress to writing words in a conventional manner.

Stage 1: Prealphabetic

This first stage, characterized by three unique levels of writing that lack any use of letter-sound connections (Paulson et al., 2001), typically occurs between the ages of 2 to 5 and includes:

1. Scribbling (irregular, horizontal, wavy lines):

2. Mock letters (individual marks made in an attempt to resemble letters):

3. Random letter strings (multiple letters written without any letter-sound connection):

Stage 2: Semiphonetic

This stage takes place when children develop an early understanding of the alphabetic principle or a beginning awareness of the connection between alphabet letters and the speech sounds that the letters represent. This stage may begin to emerge in children in the late preschool years and into kindergarten.

Chapter 4

Stage 3: Phonetic

This stage, which is typical in kindergarten and first grade, occurs when children are taught the alphabetic principle and write words using a close letter-sound correspondence.

SPAS ROKIT [space rocket]

Stage 4: Transitional

This stage, typical of second to third grade, occurs when writing is just about correct and reflects a well-developed understanding of the alphabetic principle and the written structures of print.

Pleese pass the pees.

Stage 5: Conventional

This final stage occurs when writing is orthographically and grammatically correct. The grade level that is reflective of this stage varies, depending on the complexity of the writing, but is certainly apparent in the later elementary grades.

Please pass the peas.

Table 4.2 summarizes the five stages of writing development and the age/grade ranges of progression.

Table 4.2 Typical Writing Development Progression in Young Children

Writing Development Stage	Age/Grade Range
Stage 1. Prealphabetic or Preconventional	
• Scribbling	2–3 years
• Mock letters	3–4 years
• Random letter strings	4–5 years
Stage 2. Semiphonetic or Early Alphabetic	4–6 years
Stage 3. Phonetic or Later Alphabetic	Kindergarten–Grade 1
Stage 4. Transitional	Grade 2–Grade 3
Stage 5. Conventional	Later grades

The earlier stages of print development are the focus in the early childhood years. We help children learn to distinguish between drawing and writing and move from scribbles to letter-like markings, letters, and on to producing some sound correspondences with increasing complexity.

Written Language Connections

Exercise 4.3: Identify the Levels of Writing Development

- Look at each writing sample, and identify the level of print development it represents.

Example 1

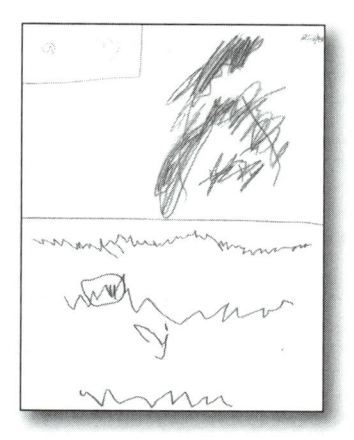

His face got away. Him teeth got away. Him ...

Example 2

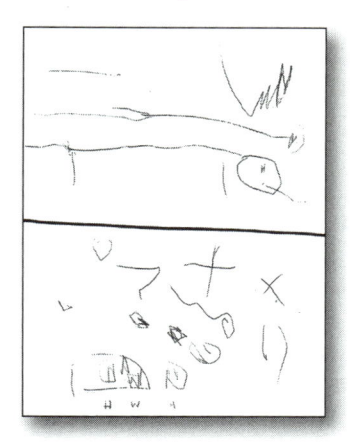

The lizard bited the snake.

(continued)

Exercise 4.3 (continued)

Example 3

We are playing a game to find these things: a ghost, my bed and tepee.

Example 4

Rainbows

Example 5

One day I was sitting in a moving truck when I was moving.

Example 6

One day we had baby guinea pigs.

Ways to Help Young Children Understand the Importance of Print

Adults model how print is used for a variety of purposes, helping children learn about written words and symbols in the environment. Through their play, children imitate adults, explore how to use print, and construct their own knowledge of written expression. When we intentionally model how print works at a child's level, we help guide learning by taking children from one stage to the next in their understanding of print.

"Picture Story/Word Story" Strategy

A strategy called Picture Story/Word Story (Paulson et al., 2001) can be used to engage young children in writing by demonstrating for them the developmental levels of writing.

This approach helps children feel comfortable writing at their own level and helps them move onto the next level. The focal element of this technique is modeling the level of print that is just *above* the level of each child in the group. If you collect writing samples prior to presenting this activity, you can group children according to their level and then scaffold children at their level. This technique easily transfers to many types of writing activities.

You can model this technique for a whole group using chart paper or for a small group at a tabletop activity using regular paper. Here are the general steps for using this technique:

1. Draw a horizontal line across the middle of the paper, visually dividing it in half.
2. Describe the concepts *top, bottom, half, center,* and *middle* to children.
3. Explain that the top half of the page will be the "Picture Story" and the bottom half will be the "Word Story." (The "Picture Story" serves to create a writing plan or what you are going to write about, and the "Word Story" is what you write.)
4. Draw a picture on the top half of the page that is related to a recent activity (e.g., reading a book, going on a field trip, coming inside from an outside activity, completing a project).
5. Write a simple sentence on the bottom half that describes the picture. Demonstrate the levels of print development by writing the same sentence in any of these forms:
    a. *Conventional manner*: Say the words aloud as you write them. Write the sentence correctly, using capital and lowercase letters, and ending with a period (e.g., "I like cookies."). Read the sentence while tracking left to right with your index finger.
        * Then say, "This is how grown-ups write. Here's another way to write. If you know the sounds the letters make, you could write your story like this: _____ ."
    b. *Phonetic manner*: Say the sounds in the words aloud while writing the sentence phonetically, and emphasize the beginning and ending sounds in the words. Do this by using "thinking aloud": demonstrate how you say a word, think about the sounds, and choose the letter that can be used for each sound as you write the word. Write the sentence correctly, using capital and lowercase letters, and ending with a period (e.g., "I lik cukez."). Read the sentence while tracking left to right with your index finger.
        * Then say, "If you know *some* of your letter sounds, you could write your story like this: _____ ."

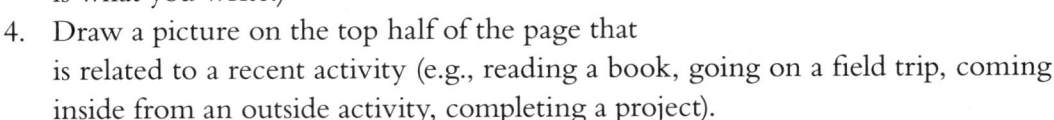

c. *Semiphonetic manner*: Say the words aloud, emphasizing the beginning sounds. Write an uppercase letter for each beginning sound, describing how you are thinking about the other sounds in the words. Write the sentence, using capital letters for the beginning sounds and ending the sentence with a period (e.g., "I L--- K---."). Read the sentence while tracking left to right with your index finger.
- Then say, "If you know a *few* letters, such as the letters in your name, you could write your story like this: _____ ."

d. *Random letter strings*: Using random letter strings, say the *letter* names while writing the sentence. Use familiar letters like **X** and **O**, and letters in the children's names (e.g., MDXXOOMX). End the sentence with a period. Read the sentence, tracking left to right with your index finger.
- Then say, "If you are not sure of *any* letters yet, you could write your story like this: _____ ."

e. *Mock letters*: Say the sentence aloud while writing letter-like squiggles or marks. End the sentence with a period. Read the sentence, tracking left to right with your index finger.
- Then say, "Here's another way you can write _____ ."

f. *Scribbles*: Say the sentence aloud while writing wavy lines horizontally in a scribble. End the sentence with a period. Read the sentence, tracking left to right with your index finger.

(The goal of Step 5 is to model writing at the level just *above* the writing level of each child in the group. Adjust the steps according to children's needs, levels of writing experience, and attention span. Although the steps are modeled swiftly, the more animated you are in delivering the directions, the longer the children's engagement and attention span may be.)

6. Have children make up their own Picture Story/Word Story. Encourage them to write using their "kid," or temporary, writing by scaffolding their understanding of how words work, identifying the letter sounds, and choosing the letters that represent the sounds. When children complete their stories, have them read their sentences to you or another adult. If their words are not recognizable, write the child's story on the back of the page.

Remember, engaging children in the act of figuring out how to identify what letters represent specific sounds is a critical step in literacy development. As children focus on letter sounds, their awareness grows. In the process, learning to decode will be easier.

Exercise 4.4 Write at Different Levels of Print

- On a sheet of paper, write this sentence: *I want to see an elephant.*
- Rewrite the sentence using these different levels of print:

   1. **Phonetic** (Listen to the sounds in the words, and write the letters that match those sounds.)
   _____

   2. **Semiphonetic** (Write the letter for the most recognizable sound in each word.)
   _____

   3. **Random letter strings** (Write the words using your favorite letters.)
   _____

   4. **Mock letters** (Make letter-like shapes to write the words.)
   _____

   5. **Scribble** (Make wavy horizontal lines to write the words.)
   _____

Sharing Ideas

When children are drawing and writing, it is an ideal time to encourage them to share their ideas with you or with the other children at their table. Ask them to talk about what they are drawing and what they are writing about. Typically, this is not a "silent" task; although some children will ask for a word to be spelled for them, let them know they will use their "kid" writing and that any kind of writing is OK. Assessing children's writing provides useful indicators of their level of print development and their understanding of the sound structure of language. However, if you have assessed that they are approaching the semiphonetic level, you can scaffold their attempts by emphasizing and elongating the sounds that have direct letter correspondences.

Exercise 4.5 Modeling Writing

- What level(s) of print should you model for a child who is:

— Scribbling? _____

— Using mock letters? _____

— Using random letters? _____

— Writing in a semiphonetic manner? _____

What young children understand about being a writer is an important component of the whole print-development process. The process that children engage in while attempting to identify the sounds in words and the letter(s) that can be used to represent the sounds is a powerful and valuable means of helping preschoolers gain a deeper understanding of the alphabetic principle. Young children need opportunities to write using their "kid" writing. They also need opportunities to dictate stories for us to write for them, to write letters to learn how to shape them, and to write their names and simple everyday words. By providing these print opportunities, we help young children develop the early literacy skills they need for a strong writing foundation.

Wrap-Up

Print is everywhere in our lives. A central goal during the preschool years is to heighten children's understanding of how print works. The three elements that make up our understanding of print include an awareness of how print works, an understanding of the written symbols that represent our spoken language, and learning to be a writer.

Children learn to recognize print, give it meaning, and use it for a variety of purposes. During the preschool years, children learn about the symbols of our alphabet and how to use them. Important to this process is having young children write *with* us, modeling for them the next stage in their learning. Children develop awareness and understanding of literacy through multiple, interactive exposures to print.

Reflection and Review

1. Describe the three components of print knowledge.

_____
_____
_____

Chapter 4

2. What skills do children need to learn in order to understand the alphabetic principle?

3. Describe the five stages and characteristics of writing development.

4. What are developmentally appropriate ways to facilitate the development of print knowledge in young children?

Chapter 5: Assessment Connections

This chapter looks at assessment, including: (a) the types of assessments that are available; (b) the purpose and importance of screening tests, and; (c) the target indicator skills and behaviors that identify what children have learned, what they need to learn, and at what point they are in the literacy learning process.

Learner Objectives for Chapter 5
- Describe the varied purposes and importance of assessment.
- Describe the different types of assessments and their intended purpose.
- Describe language and early literary behaviors that predict later literacy learning.
- Match assessment information to goals for early literacy instruction.

Warm-Up
- What are your thoughts about these questions? Jot down a response to each.
    1. What does your assessment procedure look like?

    2. How often do you use assessment procedures?

    3. What do the results of the assessments you use tell you about your young students and/or your program?

    4. What is the difference between *norm-referenced* and *criterion-referenced* assessment?

    5. What characteristics do standardized tests have?

6. What are some behaviors young children display that predict their literacy learning?

_____
_____

What Is Assessment?

The development of early literacy skills in young children is too important to allow a "wait and see" approach. As we have already discussed, children who get off to a poor start in reading rarely catch up (Torgesen, 1998). The longer we wait to intervene with a child who is not learning at the expected rate, the harder it becomes to close the gap. Having an assessment procedure based on scientific reading research is a vital component of high-quality early childhood programs. Early childhood educators need to know as much as possible about the strengths, needs, and interests of the children in their program in order to plan effective and engaging activities within a challenging and achievable curriculum in both whole-group and individual configurations.

Exercise 5.1 What Assessments Do You Use?

- Brainstorm and list all the types of assessments you use for your students.

_____
_____
_____
_____
_____

Assessment, one of the most important aspects of teaching, is an ongoing and dynamic process that includes collecting, documenting, and synthesizing information about students from a variety of sources as well as observing and interpreting student performance. The assessment process has a range of purposes; different kinds of assessments provide different types of information and are inextricably tied to instruction and intervention. Assessment is a *means to improving instruction*, not an end in itself.

Assessment is a *process*, not an event.

Appropriately developed assessment procedures have a number of purposes in the preschool classroom (see *Table 5.1*). We assess children to identify and support what they know and what they need to learn. We use assessments to identify children who are not learning at an appropriate rate and to gather information that will guide our program planning and decision-making. We use the information to document and evaluate how effective our programs are in teaching children. Assessment information also is used to report and communicate with others to identify professional development needs (Strickland & Riley-Ayers, 2006).

Table 5.1 Purposes of Preschool Assessment

- Identify and support what children know and what they need to learn.
- Identify children who are not developing at the expected rate.
- Guide program planning and instruction.
- Document and evaluate program effectiveness.
- Report and communicate with others.
- Identify professional development needs.

Characteristics of Good Assessments

Effective assessments are practical, cost-efficient, and have a reasonable level of reliability. In addition, they are validated for specific purposes and used for those purposes. Types of assessments include screening measures, diagnostic measures, progress-monitoring measures, and informal surveys and checklists of children's behavior.

Reliability of an assessment is the degree to which an assessment will elicit a consistent response pattern from a child; that is, a reliable assessment is one that yields results that represent how the child usually performs. The results are a good indicator of what that child can do on a typical day. If an assessment is reliable, you would likely get the same result if you were able to administer it several times in close sequence. It is sometimes challenging to obtain reliable assessment results for young children, as their performance may be affected by their familiarity with the assessment procedure or task, their emotional state, and their attention span. In addition, young children are learning at a rapid but uneven rate, with spurts and plateaus, and they are influenced by experience. Assessment of early literacy skills of young children who are difficult to assess and who are not responding consistently during formalized testing should be conducted by knowledgeable, experienced, and responsive professionals; otherwise, the results will not mean very much.

Validity is how well a test truly measures a particular skill or ability (construct validity) and how well it predicts future performance (predictive validity). For example, a valid measure of letter knowledge is to show alphabet letters to children and have them name them within a specified time limit. In contrast, seeing how much of the alphabet song they can sing is not a valid measure of their ability to recognize and name letters. It is well proven in research studies (NIFL, 2007) that the number of letters that 4- and 5-year-old children can name is one important valid predictor or indicator of their later literacy learning.

Why Assessment Is Important

Professional Accountability

Assessing what young children know and what they have learned, as well as documenting the effectiveness of a program, helps us be accountable. When establishing an assessment procedure, the National Institute for Early Education Research (NIEER; Strickland & Riley-Ayers, 2006) recommends that:

- The measures included in an assessment must be reliable, valid, and appropriate for the children being assessed.
- A system of analysis is established so that screening, progress-monitoring, and diagnostic test scores are interpreted as part of a broader assessment process that may include observation, portfolios, or ratings from teachers and/or parents.
- Decisions based on evaluation data reflect all aspects of children's development to include cognitive, communication, emotional, social, cultural, and physical domains.
- Teachers and parents are involved in the assessment process so that children's behaviors and abilities can be understood in various contexts and so that cooperative relationships between families and school staff can be fostered.
- Early childhood educators are provided with the professional development needed to understand and interpret the assessment results.

Early Identification of Difficulties

Early identification holds the key to early intervention that will help children who are at risk for academic learning difficulties. Young children, whose brains are still growing at a rapid pace, can be very responsive to appropriate stimulation and instruction. At the preschool level, much less time is needed to "close the gap" in vocabulary, speech-sound awareness, language comprehension, or other critical foundations. When young children are taught foundation skills for reading, writing, and language development, they are much less likely to fall behind or experience failure.

Recent research has documented the impact of early intervention on later literacy learning and has enabled us to predict later reading achievement from fairly simple and economical infant and preschool measures. Some of these findings include (Scarborough, 2002, p. 101):

- Ratings of early language milestones in children birth to 2 years predict later reading achievement better than do perceptual-motor measures.
- Preschool language abilities predict school-age outcomes and subsequent achievement.
- Verbal skills are good predictors of kindergarten-age differences in phonological awareness, letter knowledge, print concepts, and other relevant skills.
- At the youngest ages, syntactic and speech production abilities are more predictive of academic outcomes, while later in preschool, vocabulary and phonological awareness are more predictive.

- Children with a family history of reading disability remain at high risk for developing reading problems at a later age.
- Some children with early language deficits do not develop reading disabilities, and some children with reading disabilities do not display early language deficits.

Predictors of Later Literacy Difficulties

Early language characteristics and behaviors can be indicators for possible difficulties in developing reading and writing (Goldsworthy 1998; Snowling & Stackhouse 1996). Although the causal relationship has not been firmly established, many children who have had language difficulties and also difficulties with literacy development tend to display the characteristics as listed in *Table 5.2*.

Table 5.2 Early Language Indicators for Later Literacy Difficulties

Age	Difficulty Indicator
2½ years	• Produces only short, simple sentences • Has less accurate word production
3 years	• Displays receptive language problems • Has difficulty naming items, objects, people • May have phonological pattern problems (e.g., faulty pronunciation of words)
4 years	• May not know the boundaries between words • Has problems differentiating similar-sounding words • Has problems distinguishing and producing complex words
5 years	• Poor word recall • Poor letter and letter-sound knowledge • Poor rhyming • Poor phonemic awareness

- **2 ½ Years Old**

    At this age, in contrast to normally progressing children, those at risk for later problems may use short, simple sentences. Their word production may be noticeably inaccurate. They often display some difficulty in figuring out the structure of language and use mainly single-word utterances. They use a limited number of vocabulary words, and a small number of speech sounds, typically /b/, /m/, and /d/.

- **3 Years Old**

    Children at this age who are at risk for later problems may have difficulty understanding language, difficulty naming common objects accurately (e.g., saying *cow* for "horse," *sit-down thing* for "chair," *fork* for "spoon"), and/or have speech patterns that are difficult to understand (phonological patterning problems).

- **4 Years Old**
  Children at this age who are at risk for later reading and academic problems may have trouble detecting and/or articulating word boundaries (e.g., saying *neck store* for "next door"); may produce sentences that are noticeably different from anything they have heard others say, and may put words together strangely (e.g., saying *she-her going to-a store* for "she is going to the store"). Also, they may often have trouble differentiating between similar-sounding words and producing complex sound clusters and words (e.g., saying *alligator* for "elevator" or *pasgetii* for "spaghetti").

- **5 Years Old**
  Children entering kindergarten who are at risk for later problems may have word-finding problems (i.e., trouble recalling from memory the word they want to say), poor letter naming, poor letter-sound association, poor rhyming skills, and limited phonological awareness.

Assessment Characteristics and Scores

Assessments are designed for specific purposes, which give them different characteristics. Some assessments may be norm-referenced or criterion-referenced, some may be standardized, and some are informal. In general, most measures produce a raw score, which is typically the number of items answered correctly or, in the case of informal measures, the number of items observed. Raw scores are typically converted into other scores that are more meaningful in determining where a child stands in relation to an age-level or grade-level expectation. The type of score conversion depends on the type of assessment; refer to *Appendix B* for definitions and descriptions of scores and score components.

- **Norm-referenced** assessments compare a child's performance to a normative sample of children the same age or grade level. Raw scores obtained from this type of assessment are generally converted to scores of relative standing, including percentile ranks, standard scores, and age/grade equivalent scores.

- **Criterion-referenced** assessments compare a child's performance (or other attribute) to a benchmark or functional level of performance. For example, a criterion-referenced measure of motor skill development would check whether a student met age-level criteria on a series of structured tasks (e.g., throwing a ball, cutting paper with scissors, climbing stairs, performing jumping jacks). The scores are often expressed as a percentage of correct responses (e.g., the number of observed or not observed responses as a function of the total number of responses). Criterion-referenced scores are intuitive and easy to understand because they tell you how many items or responses the child gave correctly in relation to the number that is typically expected of a child at a specified level of development. Criterion-referenced tests are not norm-referenced (i.e., they do not yield a percentile rank).

Note: There is a distinct difference between percentage scores in criterion-referenced scoring and percentile scoring in norm-referenced assessments. A percentile rank tells us where a child would be ranked among 100 other children on a specific skill. For example, a child at the 68th percentile is better at that skill than 68 children out of 100. A percentage, however, tells us what proportion of a total set of tasks the child accomplished.

- **Standardized** assessments, a more formal type, are designed to be given the same way each time so that the assessment scores will be reliable. They are designed to efficiently sample a child's skills within a prescribed domain *under controlled conditions*. These assessments can be either norm-referenced or criterion-referenced. In general, examiners must be trained and supervised so that they administer assessments objectively and reliably while engaging students in specified tasks. Examples of standardized assessments for young children include:
    - *Expressive One-Word Picture Vocabulary Test* (EOWPVT; Brownell, 2000)
    - *Peabody Picture Vocabulary Test* (3rd ed.) (PPVT-III; Dunn & Dunn, 1997)
    - *Test of Preschool Early Literacy* (TOPEL; Lonigan, Wagner, Torgesen, & Rashotte, 2007)
    - *Preschool Language Scale* (4th ed.) (PLS-4; Zimmerman, Steiner, & Pond, 2002)
- **Informal** assessments include methods such as observations, portfolios, teacher ratings, and parent ratings. The use of observation and teacher rating scales alone is *not* sufficient to identify children's level of learning in relation to age-level or grade-level norms. During informal assessments and observations, children may not have opportunities to display specific skills that predict future levels of learning. Informal assessments are often completed while observing children in their natural environments and, although informal assessments do add valuable information, they should not be the only assessment methods used.

Four Types of Formal Assessments for Young Children

An effective assessment approach in a preschool program includes the use of several kinds of assessments designed for specific purposes. Each of these types of assessments generally use standardized procedures and may be either norm-referenced or criterion-referenced.

- **Screening** assessments are used to identify children's general levels of learning in relation to a "benchmark" standard. Screening should be used simply to roughly identify children who are developing within average levels and those who appear to be at risk for later difficulties.

- **Progress-monitoring** assessments are used to monitor children's progress or growth on basic skills such as naming letters, naming common objects, or producing words that are being emphasized in the curriculum and that are part of a core vocabulary.
- **Diagnostic** assessments are used to determine children's individual unique strengths and weaknesses.
- **Outcome** assessments are used to document and evaluate the effectiveness of literacy programs in preparing children for formal schooling.

All four of these types of assessments produce a variety of scores and results, which provide efficient, effective, and objective ways of characterizing children's skills, learning levels, or abilities (see *Table 5.3*). However, scores may be tricky to understand. There are a number of concepts and issues that must be understood if scores are to be used effectively. One of the most important concepts for the appropriate interpretation of scores is to understand that they are only estimates of the attribute or domain of interest (e.g., phonological awareness). We describe some fundamental concepts that are necessary to understand scores in *Appendix B*.

Table 5.3 Types of Formal Assessments and Related Functions

Screening	Identify children who are—and are not—learning at an expected level.
Progress-monitoring	Monitor the progress or growth of children receiving specialized instruction.
Diagnostic	Determine children's individual strengths and weaknesses.
Outcome	Document and evaluate the effectiveness of literacy programs.

Screening Assessments

Screening assessments are used to efficiently determine which children are learning at the expected rate and, conversely, those who are not. Importantly, the results of screening tests must have a high level of predictive validity; that is, the results should unquestionably identify children who are likely to have trouble learning to read, write, or handle language and academic tasks in the future, beyond the pre-K or kindergarten level. Because screenings are designed to make general predictions, they are not in-depth or lengthy assessments. Screenings should: (a) be brief; (b) involve all children; and (c) be conducted three or four times throughout the school year—often at the beginning (September), mid-year (January), and the end (April or May). Screening procedures are given under standardized conditions and may be either norm-referenced or criterion-referenced. If a screening procedure is developed by a teacher or a program, the directions and scoring criteria should be standardized so that every person who uses the screening is likely to come up with reliable results. Comparisons of children to each other or to themselves over time are impossible unless assessment measures are given in a standardized manner.

Analyzing screening results from all children in your program can provide information about whether the expected and desired learning outcomes are being achieved. These results document that children who participate in a particular program or who receive a particular instructional strategy are learning the skills we want them to be learning at a rate that is appropriate for their age. Analyses help to identify how well a program is meeting its goals and also where a program needs improvement and what kind of professional development would be most important for teachers. A few widely used published early literacy screening assessments include:

- **Get Ready to Read!® Screening Tool**
  National Center for Learning Disabilities (NCLD)
  Web site: http://www.getready to read.org
  The *Get Ready to Read! Screening Tool* is a 20-item, computer-based online instrument that focuses on the skill areas of print knowledge, emergent writing, and linguistic awareness of children in the year before they enter kindergarten. This tool consists of a reliable, research-based series of questions to determine whether pre-kindergarten children have the early literacy skills they will need to become readers.

- **Individual Growth and Development Indicators (IGDI)**
  University of Minnesota Web site: http://ggg.umn.edu
  IGDIs are quick, efficient, and repeatable measures of the components of developmental performance. The early literacy measures include rhyme matching, alliteration matching, and picture naming. These indicators measure young children's growth over time toward important developmental outcomes rather than just their skill level at one point in time. Preschool IGDIs are intended for children between the chronological ages of 30 months and 6 years of age. This type of screening assessment may be administered to monitor children's progress, to identify children who might benefit from specialized intervention, and to monitor the effects of such intervention. IGDI directions, stimulus pictures, and protocols are available online.

- **Phonological Awareness Literacy Screening (PALS™-PreK and PALS™-K)**
  PALS-PreK Web site: http://pals.virginia.edu/tools-prek.html
  PALS-K Web site: http://pals.virginia.edu/tools-k.html
  PALS Pre-K and K literacy screening tools measure young children's knowledge of rhyme, awareness of beginning sounds, the ability to name letters of the alphabet, familiarity with books and print, and name-writing. This screening assessment identifies children's literacy strengths as well as literacy areas that may require more attention.

Progress-Monitoring Assessments

Progress-monitoring assessments are designed to be used with children who have been identified in the screening process as not learning at the expected rate. These children may need more instruction on particular skills, more practice, or a different approach to learning the skills. Children's progress should be monitored using the same screening method after a short instructional period (i.e., several weeks) of the target skills to see what learning has occurred. The results also should be used to determine if the intervention is helping children make adequate progress in their learning or if they need more assistance to achieve the expected outcomes to keep their learning on track.

Progress-monitoring assessments consist of multiple forms of the same task to reliably measure children's learning progress. An IGDI is an example of a progress-monitoring assessment and has a series of rhyme-matching pictures that can be used without repeating the items in previous administrations of the screening. Multiple forms of series allow for more reliable results and limit the influence of the practice effect that can occur when the same items are used within a short period of time.

Diagnostic Assessments

Diagnostic assessments have two purposes; first, they are used to identify strengths and specific needs of children who display significant delays in their development. This information can then be used to target areas of instruction (e.g., vocabulary, letter recognition, phonological awareness) and to identify unique learning problems within the target areas. Second, diagnostic assessments are used to classify an area of disability. In-depth diagnostic assessments that are used for classification of disability are most often conducted by team members as part of a referral for special education. A few examples of published early literacy diagnostic assessments include:

- **Assessment of Literacy and Language (ALL)**—Pearson Education, Inc.
  This diagnostic assessment is used to assess spoken language and written language skills, including listening comprehension, language comprehension, semantics, syntax, phonological awareness, alphabetic principle/phonics, and concepts about print. ALL can help to identify language disorders, language and emergent literacy deficits, emergent literacy deficits, and weak language and emergent literacy at pre-kindergarten through first-grade levels.

- **Test of Early Reading Ability (3rd ed.) (TERA3)**—Pro-Ed
  This diagnostic assessment is a direct measure of reading ability of young children ages 3-6 through 8-6, assessing their mastery of early developing reading skills. Three subtests include alphabet knowledge and uses, conventions of print, and print meaning. Standard scores are provided for each subtest. An overall Reading Quotient is computed using all three subtest scores.

- **Test of Preschool Early Literacy (TOPEL)**—Pro-Ed
  This diagnostic assessment is designed for identifying 3- to 5-year-old preschoolers who are at risk for literacy challenges. The Print Knowledge subtest includes alphabet knowledge and early knowledge about written language conventions and form. The Definitional Vocabulary subtest measures single-word oral vocabulary and definitional vocabulary, which assesses both surface and deep vocabulary knowledge. The Phonological Awareness subtest measures word elision and blending abilities. *TOPEL* provides valid and reliable raw scores, standard scores, and percentiles. *TOPEL* provides educators and researchers with a reliable and valid means of:
  (a) monitoring children's progress toward proficient literacy; (b) identifying children who need focused intervention; (c) evaluating the impacts of educational programs; and (d) identifying key developmental experiences that enhance children's progress.

Outcome Assessments

Outcome assessments are designed to document and evaluate the effectiveness of instructional programs, individually or overall. Of course, the process of evaluating educational programs can range from informal to complex and statistically sophisticated. Informal program evaluations may simply rely on comparing the beginning and end-of-year performance of children on an outcome measure. The results from outcome assessments, administered in September and May (i.e., the beginning and end of the school year) can be compared to see how much children have learned, what areas were strong, and what areas were not as developed. Complex program evaluations are typically intertwined with research and evaluation methodologies.

Table 5.4 summarizes the early literacy assessments we have discussed, along with the function of each.

Table 5.4 Examples of Early Literacy Assessments and Their Characteristics

Standardized Assessments	N-R	C-R	S	PM	D	O
Get Ready to Read!®		X	X			—
Individual Growth and Development Indicators (IGDI)		X	X	X		—
Phonological Awareness Literacy Screening (PALS™-PreK and PALS™-K)		X	X	X		—
Assessment of Literacy and Language (ALL)	X				X	—
Test of Early Reading Ability (3rd ed.) (TERA3)	X				X	—
Test of Preschool Early Literacy (TOPEL)	X				X	—

N-R=Norm-Referenced; C-R=Criterion-Referenced; S=Screening; PM =Progress-Monitoring; D=Diagnostic; O=Outcome

Types of Informal Assessments

Observations and *teacher ratings* are often structured to compare a student with a developmental scale and usually involve the use of some type of checklist. Observations of children's behaviors are typically made in a natural, familiar environment (i.e., home or school) and enable the observer to document incidences of skill use.

Portfolios contain multiple sources and methods of data collection and accumulate over a period of time. A collection of children's work provides rich documentation of their progress over the course of a school year. A portfolio can prove to be treasure trove of valuable information about a child's performance that can be easily shared among parents, teachers, and other staff. Portfolios also provide means to integrate assessment information with tangible results of instruction and learning.

Parent ratings assist families in observing and listening to their children. This process provides important information about children's achievement of developmental milestones, their typical behaviors, and indications of what skills should be next to develop.

These methods and sources are important pieces of the assessment process, even though the techniques used are informal and do not involve standard scores, percentiles, or grade equivalents. If you create your own assessment procedure, you can establish your own local norms to give your results more meaning. Standardized procedures must be established for gathering information on a checklist or a rating scale, for establishing interobserver reliability, and for judging observed behaviors. We describe this process in *Appendix C*.

Examples of Published Informal Assessment Measures

- **Early Language and Literacy Classroom Observation (ELLCO)**
  Web site: http://www.brookespublising.com/store/books/smithellco/index.htm
  ELLCO is a pre-kindergarten through third grade classroom observation tool that specifically addresses the role of environmental factors in early literacy and language development. It is useful for conducting a baseline assessment as well as for determining progress in providing learning environments that are age appropriate, support children's evolving interests, and that engage children in exploring beyond their existing knowledge and skills.

Exercise 5.2 — Categorize Your Assessments

- Refer back to the answers you gave to question #2 in the Warm-Up section.
- Of the assessments you listed, which ones are characteristically:

  — Norm-referenced? _____

  — Criterion-referenced? _____

  — Standardized and/or informal? _____

- What types of assessment are they? (check all that apply)

  ○ Screening   ○ Progress-monitoring   ○ Diagnostic   ○ Outcome

- Does your assessment process include each of these types of assessments?

  ○ Yes   ○ No

Exercise 5.3 Identify the Type of Assessment

1. At the beginning of the school year, 15 children in your 4-year-old group looked at a series of picture sets to identify the words that rhyme. According to the authors of the assessment, children at this age are on track to successful early reading if they correctly identify 60 percent or more of the rhyming pairs. Five of your children correctly identified all of the rhyming word pairs, and ten did not, scoring "below benchmark" (i.e., below the level that predicts later success).

   - What type of assessment is this? _____
   - What do the results tell you?

   _____

   _____

   - What do the results *not* tell you?

   _____

   _____

   - What should you do after getting this information?

   _____

   _____

   _____

2. After conducting rhyming activities for several weeks, you administer the same assessment, having the ten "below benchmark" children look at the picture sets to assess their rhyme-matching skills. This time, five of those children were consistently able to match the word pairs that rhyme.

   - What type of assessment is this? _____
   - What do the results tell you, and what do you need to do?

   _____

   _____

3. Of the five children who were not learning to rhyme, three are making some gains in their rhyming ability; however, two do not seem to be making any gains. These two children also have underdeveloped skills in several other areas.

   - What should you do? _____

   _____

The Early Literacy Checklist

As we have discussed, the three early literacy foundations are oral language, phonological awareness, and print knowledge. Skills in each of these areas need to be assessed to identify how children are developing so that we can provide appropriate instruction at an adequate level to meet their individual needs.

The Early Literacy Checklist (ELC; see next page), adapted from *Building Early Literacy and Language Skills* (BELLS; Paulson et al., 2001), is a tool that can be used by early childhood educators, parents, and caregivers to informally identify the general level of early literacy skill development of young children. The ELC is designed to provide information in the areas of oral language, phonological awareness, and print knowledge. It can be used as part of an assessment procedure to identify a child's level of skill development and later to document the child's progress and growth. The items on the ELC provide a guideline for determining which skills have been acquired, which skills can be enhanced, and which skills need to be developed.

The specific assessment dates can be noted at the top of the form. Also, the dates that skills were observed can be written on the lines preceding the specific items. It is particularly important to identify skill areas that are not developing at an expected rate, especially those skills that are predictive of future difficulties with reading and writing. When delays are identified, you can initiate appropriate interventions to facilitate the development of those skills.

The skills listed in the "Oral Language" section of the ELC help to identify those that correspond to the language structures described in Chapter 2. Children's speech intelligibility is a measure of their phonological development. Concept understanding is a measure of vocabulary. Using correct word order and sentence structures is a measure of how syntax is developing; the use of word endings measures morphology. Relating events identifies a child's sense of telling a story.

Early Literacy Checklist

Name of student: _____ Birth date: _____

Teacher: _____

Assessment dates: _____, _____, _____, _____, _____

Oral Language
_____ Uses speech that is understandable with only age-appropriate errors
_____ Understands concepts such as *top/bottom, under/over, beginning/middle/end, first/last/next, before/after, one/all, more/less, same/not same*
_____ Uses word endings that indicate plurals, possessives, present tense, past tense (e.g., -s, -ing, -ed)
_____ Uses sentences with correct word order, of appropriate length, and includes pronouns, verbs, and question forms
_____ Relates a story with three to five events

Phonological Awareness
Rhyme
_____ Imitates rhythmic patterns in songs, rhymes, and fingerplays
_____ Fills in missing words to known songs, rhymes, fingerplays
_____ Identifies words that rhyme
_____ Produces a word that rhymes with a given word
_____ Produces a string of three words that rhyme

Blending
_____ Blends words into syllables (e.g., **cow-boy**)
_____ Blends the beginning sound to the rest of a word (e.g., **f-ish**)
_____ Blends words with three sounds (e.g., **s-u-n**)

Segmenting
_____ Segments words into syllables
_____ Identifies the number of syllables in words
_____ Identifies words that begin with the same sound
_____ Segments the beginning sound from the rest of a word (e.g., **s-un**)
_____ Segments sounds in words with three sounds (e.g., **h-a-t**)

Print Knowledge
Print Awareness
_____ Holds book right-side-up and turns one page at a time
_____ Identifies the pictures and words on a page
_____ Recognizes symbols and print seen in the environment
_____ Follows print using left-to-right sequencing
_____ Points to words using 1:1 word correspondence
_____ Recognizes own written name

Alphabet Knowledge
_____ Sings the "Alphabet Song"
_____ Identifies uppercase letters
_____ Identifies lowercase letters
_____ Identifies the sounds of letters
_____ Produces the sounds of letters

Writing Development
_____ Writes using scribble-like markings
_____ Writes using individual letter-like characters or mock letters
_____ Writes using recognizable, random letter strings
_____ Writes using semiphonetic spellings
_____ Writes using phonetic spellings

Copyright 2010 Cambium Learning Sopris West®. All rights reserved.
Permission is granted to reproduce this page for teacher use.

Exercise 5.4 Match the Oral Skill to the Language Structure

- Fill in the blanks with the oral language structure that matches the oral language skill.

phonology   semantics   morphology   syntax   prosody

_____	Uses speech that is understandable with only age-appropriate errors
_____	Understands concepts such as *top/bottom, under/over, beginning/middle/end, first/last/next, before/after, one/all, more/less, same/not same*
_____	Uses word endings that indicate plurals, possessives, present tense, past tense (e.g., **-s, -ing, -ed**)
_____	Uses sentences with correct word order, of appropriate length, and includes pronouns, verbs, and question forms
_____	Relates a story with three to five events

The "Phonological Awareness" section of the ELC is divided into the components of rhyme, blending, and segmenting, as described in Chapter 3 of this manual. Alliteration is not separated as an individual skill but is included as a subskill within segmenting. Each component follows a developmental sequence from easier to harder skills. The earliest developing skills occur in children as young as 2 years old; the later skills may not develop until children are in kindergarten.

Exercise 5.5 Indicate the Progression of Phonological Skills

- Underline the phonological awareness item on this list that addresses alliteration.
- What is the age expectation for each phonological awareness skill to begin to develop?

Phonological Awareness Items	Age Expectation
Rhyme	
Imitates rhythmic patterns in songs, rhymes, and fingerplays	_____
Fills in missing words to known songs, rhymes, and fingerplays	_____
Identifies words that rhyme	_____
Produces a word that rhymes with a given word	_____
Produces a string of three words that rhyme	_____
Blending	
Blends words into syllables (e.g., **cow-boy**)	_____
Blends the beginning sound to the rest of a word (e.g., **f-ish**)	_____
Blends words with three sounds (e.g., **s-u-n**)	_____
Segmenting	
Segments words into syllables	_____
Identifies the number of syllables in words	_____
Identifies words that begin with the same sound	_____
Segments the beginning sound from the rest of a word (e.g., **s-un**)	_____
Segments sounds in words with three sounds (e.g., **h-a-t**)	_____

The three components of the "Print Knowledge" section of the ELC are represented as described in Chapter 4. Each of the listed skills follows a general progression of development in the areas of print awareness, alphabet knowledge, and being a writer.

Exercise 5.6   Match Checklist Items to Your Assessments

- Which of your assessment procedures addresses each item in the "Oral Language," "Phonological Awareness," and "Print Knowledge" sections of the Early Literacy Checklist?

_____

_____

_____

_____

_____

This Early Literacy Checklist provides a guide to the skills that young children learn that will support their literacy learning. Within your comprehensive assessment procedure, you also need to assess other developmental areas, including motor skills, mathematical and thinking skills, and social skills, which are intricately related to language development.

Wrap-Up

Assessment is one of the most important responsibilities that early childhood educators have. The assessment continuum includes using observations and checklists as well as standardized norm-referenced and criterion-referenced procedures to identify what children know and what they need to learn. This information is critical for: (a) early identification of literacy deficits; (b) planning and instruction; (c) evaluating program effectiveness; (d) communicating with others; and (e) identifying professional development needs.

Target skills in each of the early literacy foundations have been identified. Knowing what these areas are and having a plan to assess them is a component of high-quality early childhood settings.

Reflection and Review

1. List the purposes and uses of assessment.

_____

_____

_____

_____

2. What are predictive behaviors that foretell reading development?

3. Describe the characteristics of both *norm-referenced* and *criterion-referenced* assessments.

4. Describe both *informal* and *standardized* assessments.

5. Describe the components of your assessment procedure that identify children's early literacy skills.

Glossary

alliteration: the identification and production of words that begin with the same sound (e.g., <u>b</u>ig, <u>b</u>right, <u>b</u>lue, <u>b</u>utterfly)

alphabetic principle: the principle that letters are used to represent individual phonemes in the spoken word; a critical foundational insight for beginning reading and spelling

assembly: the fourth stage of language development in which children add endings (e.g., **-s**, **-ed**, **-ing**) to words in sentences

assessment: an ongoing and dynamic process that includes collecting, documenting, and synthesizing information as well as observing and interpreting student performance

babbling: an early stage of language development characterized by vocalizations, usually in a consonant-vowel-consonant-vowel (CVCV) pattern, with no word meaning (e.g., "babababa")

blending: the act of putting phonemes, onset-rime patterns, and/or syllables together to make a whole word (e.g., hearing /k/ /ă/ /t/, then saying **cat**). *Oral blending* involves speech only, while *phonic blending* involves assembly of letter-sounds in a printed word.

cognates: pairs of speech sounds that are produced in the same place in the mouth, but one sound is voiceless and the other sound is voiced (e.g., /th/ and /<u>th</u>/)

context processor: the neural networks that bring background knowledge and discourse to bear as word meanings are processed

continuant sounds: speech sounds that can be produced for longer periods of time (e.g., /f/, /v/, /th/, /s/, /z/, /sh/, /zh/, /h/)

conventional print development: written language with correct spelling, punctuation, and grammar

diagnostic assessments: assessments used to identify strengths and specific needs of students who display a significant delay in their development

dialogic storybook reading: a method of shared reading in which an adult helps a child become a storyteller by asking the child questions about the text

early alphabetic stage: a stage of written language development characterized by semi-phonetic spellings (e.g., *wgn* = **wagon**, *lv* = **love**). This stage occurs when a child has a beginning understanding of the alphabetic principle.

early literacy: in young children, reading and writing behaviors with no awareness, or only a beginning awareness, of letter-sound relationships

emergent literacy perspective: an educational perspective that places a heavy value on the social and meaning-based aspects of literacy and creating a learning environment in which children can explore and learn

evidence-based reading research (EBRR) perspective: an educational perspective that focuses on a core set of knowledge and skills that young children must develop in order to become successful readers and writers, along with strategies that can be used to teach these skills through explicit instruction

expansion: a language-stimulation technique to expand children's utterances by restating them in a slightly longer form (e.g., child says, "Look, bird"; adult restates as, "You see a blue bird")

glide: a speech sound that is produced with some movement or gliding of either the lips or the tongue (e.g., /w/, /y/)

informal assessment: a form of assessment that includes methods such as observations, portfolios, teacher ratings, and parent ratings

invented spelling: a basic phonetic spelling of a word (e.g., *wn* = **one**)

later alphabetic print development: written language that is characterized by phonetic spellings (e.g., *wegn* = **wagon**, *luv* = **love**) and that occurs when there is a developed understanding of the alphabetic principle

lexic stage: a stage of language development that begins when babies (i.e., about 12 months old) say their first words

liquid: a type of speech sound that is produced as a consonant sound at the beginning of words or syllables, and as a vowel sound at the ends of words or syllables (e.g., /l/, /r/)

literacy: the process of communicating through written language

logographic stage: a stage of literacy development that begins when children recognize written symbols in their environment; also called the *prealphabetic stage*

manner: a characteristic of speech sounds that describes the way consonant sounds are produced; types of speech sounds include *stops, continuants, nasals, glides,* and *liquids*

meaning processor: an aspect of brain functioning that identifies words based on vocabulary and stored background knowledge during the reading process

metaphonological stage: a stage of language development that occurs when children realize that the words they use to communicate have a meaning and a structure that can be changed and manipulated

mock letters: a type of writing that is characterized by individual letter-like marks; this type of writing is associated with the preconventional stage of print development

morpheme: the smallest meaningful unit of language (e.g., the word **meaningful** has three morphemes, or word parts—*mean–ing–ful*—that add to its meaning)

morphology: the study and description of word formation

narrative skills: the ability to describe related events and ideas

nasal sounds: speech sounds that are produced in the nasal (nose) cavity (e.g., /m/, /n/, /ng/)

onset: the beginning consonant or consonant cluster of a one-syllable word (e.g., **s** in **sat**, **tr** in **tree**)

orthographic processor: the aspect of brain functioning that visually recognizes word patterns based on letter configurations during the reading process

orthographic stage: a stage of literacy development characterized by fluent reading, an ability to self-correct, and an ability to learn new word meanings

pausing: a scaffolding technique that allows a brief wait time to encourage students to fill in words in familiar stories or to anticipate what will come next in a story

phonemic awareness: the ability to reflect on and consciously manipulate the phonemes or speech sounds in words; a more sophisticated component of phonological awareness

phonetic stage: a stage of print development characterized by an ability to analyze sounds in words and to use simple consonant and vowel word structures when writing

phonological awareness: the awareness of the sound structures of language; the ability to reflect on and consciously manipulate syllables and sounds of speech

phonological memory: the ability to immediately recall and code sound-based information in short-term memory for temporary storage

phonological naming: the ability to efficiently retrieve phonological information, which is stored in long-term memory

phonological processing: the ability to understand and use the sound system of a language to process oral and written information

phonological processor: the aspect of brain functioning that, on a subconscious level, "pronounces" everything that is read

phonological representation: the distinctness of a given word stored in memory and the ability to access this word representation in a conscious manner

phonology: the study of the speech sounds of language and the rules used to put sounds together to say words

Glossary

prealphabetic stage: a stage of print development in which a child's writing contains no letter-sound correspondences; also called the *preconventional stage*

preconventional stage (see *prealphabetic stage*)

prelexic stage: a stage of oral language development characterized by cooing and babbling that contains no real words

prelogographic stage: a stage of literacy development that occurs before recognition or understanding of symbols or print

print awareness: a component of print knowledge that is characterized by an understanding that print is meaningful; a recognition of print in the environment

print knowledge: a foundation area of early literacy that is characterized by knowing that spoken words are represented by written symbols

progress-monitoring assessments: assessments designed to be used with students receiving additional intervention to determine what learning has occurred on target skills using the same screening method

prosody: the rhythmic and intonational aspect of spoken language

random letter strings: writing that is characterized by strings of letters to represent words without any letter-sound relationships (e.g., MSTXS); a level of writing in the *preconventional stage* of print development

reliability: the consistency of a student's performance in an assessment

rhyme: a word pattern that reflects the same sound sequence at the ends of words (e.g., **tail/pail/sale**; **hat/cat/bat**)

rime: the last syllable of a word that includes the vowel and final consonants (e.g., **-at** in **sat**; **-ee** in **tree**)

scaffolding: a teaching technique for facilitating development by encouraging student performance at successively higher and complex levels

screening assessments: assessments designed to determine which students are learning at the expected rate and those who may need additional intervention

scribble: writing characterized by wavy lines with a left-to-right orientation; a level of writing in the *preconventional stage* of print development

segmenting: dividing words into parts, including phonemes, syllables, and/or onsets and rimes (e.g., **telephone** becomes **te–le–phone**, **cat** becomes **c–a–t**)

semantics: the study of word and phrase meanings

semiphonetic: a stage of print development characterized by a beginning awareness of the relationship between letters and sounds (e.g., *wgn* = **wagon**, *lv* = **love**); also called the *early alphabetic* or *partial alphabetic stage*

sentence recasting: a scaffolding technique in which a story line is read and then repeated to facilitate understanding

speech intelligibility: the ability to accurately say the speech sounds of a language

standardized assessment: a method of assessment designed to be administered the same way each time it is given to efficiently measure skills in a prescribed body of knowledge under controlled conditions to tap a momentary level of functioning in time

stop: a type of consonant sound that is produced with a puff of air and not continued or carried out (e.g., /p/, /b/, /t/, /d/, /ch/, /j/, /k/, /g/)

story retelling: a scaffolding technique in which an adult reader summarizes a story or encourages students to retell the story

syntax: the system of grammatical rules that govern permissible word order in sentences

systematic simplification: a stage of language development characterized by word combinations in short sentences (e.g., "Mommy sock")

tag question: a scaffolding technique to facilitate understanding and to gain agreement by tagging a comment with a question ("This is red, isn't it?")

transitional: the stage of print development when a student's writing is just about correct and exhibits a well-developed understanding of the alphabetic principle and the written structures of print

validity: the degree to which an assessment truly measures a particular skill or ability and predicts future performance

verbal dialogue: a scaffolding technique to create a story based on pictures in a text

vocabulary: the bank of words that are understood and used in a language

voiced sounds: speech sounds that are pronounced with vibrations of the vocal cords (e.g., /m/, /b/, /w/, /v/, /d/, /n/, /l/, /th/, /z/, /zh/, /j/, /r/, /y/, /g/, /ng/)

voiceless sounds: speech sounds that are pronounced without vibrations of the vocal cords (e.g., /p/, /f/, /th/, /t/, /s/, /sh/, /ch/, /k/, /h/, /wh/)

word: a speech sound, or series of them, serving to communicate meaning and consisting of at least one base morpheme with or without prefixes or suffixes; the unit of language between the morpheme and the sentence

References

Adams, M. J. (2002). Alphabetic anxiety and explicit, systematic phonics instruction: A cognitive science perspective. In S. B. Neuman & D. K. Dickinson (Eds.), *Handbook of early literacy research* (pp. 66–80). New York: Guilford Press.

Adams, M. J. (1990). *Beginning to read, thinking and learning about print*. Cambridge, MA: MIT Press.

American Speech-Language-Hearing Association (ASHA). (2001). *Roles and responsibilities of speech-language pathologists with respect to reading and writing in children and adolescents*. Ad Hoc Committee on Reading and Written Language Disorders. Bethesda, MD: Author.

Anthony, J. L., & Francis, D. J. (2005). Development of phonological awareness. *American Psychology Society, 14*(5), 255–259.

Anthony, J. L., Lonigan, C. J., Burgess, S. R., Driscoll, K., Phillips, B. M., & Cantor, B. G. (2002). Structure of preschool phonological sensitivity: Overlapping sensitivity to rhyme, words, syllables, and phonemes. *Journal of Experimental Child Psychology, 82*, 65–92.

Arnold, D. H., Lonigan, C. J., Whitehurst, G. J., & Epstein, J. N. (1994). Accelerating language development through picture book reading: Replication and extension to a videotape training format. *Journal of Educational Psychology, 86*, 235–243.

Ashby, J., & Rayner, K. (2006). Literacy development: Insights from research on skilled reading. In D. K. Dickinson & S. B. Neuman (Eds.), *Handbook of early literacy research* (Vol. 2, pp. 52–63). New York: Guilford Press.

Assel, M. A., Landry, S. H., & Swank, P. R. (2007). Are early childhood classrooms preparing children to be school ready? The CIRCLE Teacher Behavior Rating Scale. In L. Justice & C. Vukelich (Eds.), *Achieving excellence in preschool literacy instruction* (pp. 120–135). New York: Guilford Press.

Assel, M. A., Landry, S. H., Swank, P. R., & Gunnewig, S. (2006). An evaluation of curriculum, setting, and mentoring on the performance of children enrolled in prekindergarten. *Reading and Writing: An Interdisciplinary Journal, 20*, 463–494.

Ball, E., & Blachman, B. (1988). Phonological segmentation training: Effects of reading readiness. *Annals of Dyslexia, 38*, 208–225.

Bauman-Waengler, J. (2009). *Introduction to phonetics and phonology: From concepts to transcription*. Boston: Pearson.

Blachman, B. (1991). *Getting ready to read: Learning how print maps to speech*. Bethesda, MD: National Institute of Child Health and Human Development (NICHD), U.S. Department of Health and Human Services.

Bowman, B. T., Donovan, M. S., & Burns, M. S. (Eds.). (2001). *Eager to learn: Educating our preschoolers*. Washington, DC: National Academy Press.

References

Bredekamp, S., & Copple, C. (Eds.). (1998). *Developmentally appropriate practice in early childhood programs* (Rev. ed.). Washington, DC: National Association for the Education of Young Children (NAEYC).

Brownell, R. (2000). *Expressive one-word picture vocabulary test* (EOWPVT). Novato, CA: Academic Therapy.

Bryant, P. E., MacLean, M., Bradley, L. L., & Crossland, J. (1990). Rhyme and alliteration, phonemic detection, and learning to read. *Developmental Psychology, 26,* 429–438.

Burgess, S. R. (2006). The development of phonological sensitivity. In D. K. Dickinson & S. B. Neuman (Eds.), *Handbook of early literacy research* (Vol. 2, pp. 90–100). New York: Guilford Press.

Byrne, B., & Fielding-Barnsley, R. (1995). Evaluation of a program to teach phonemic awareness to young children: A 2- and 3-year follow-up and a new preschool trial. *Journal of Educational Psychology, 87,* 488–503.

Carey, S. (1978). The child as word learner. In M. Halle, J. Bresnan, & G. Miller (Eds.), *Linguistic theory and psychological reality* (pp. 264–293). Cambridge, MA: MIT Press.

Casey, A., & Sheran, C. (2004). Early literacy skills development. *National Association of School Psychologists Communiqué, 32*(6). Retrieved April 3, 2009, from http://www1.rism.ac.th/2005/PA/pdf/NASPdocs/EarlyLitSkills.pdf

Catts, H. (1991). Facilitating phonological awareness: Role of speech-language pathologists. *Language, Speech, and Hearing Services in Schools, 22*(4), 196–203.

CTB/McGraw-Hill. (1990). *Developing skills checklist.* Monterey, CA: Author.

Dickinson, D. K., & Smith, M. W. (1994). Long-term effects of preschool teachers' book reading on low-income children's vocabulary and story comprehension. *Reading Research Quarterly, 29,* 104–122.

Dickinson, D. K., & Tabors, P. O. (2001). *Beginning literacy with language.* Baltimore: Paul H. Brookes.

Duncan, G. J., Dowsett, C. J., Claessens, A., Magnuson, K., Huston, A. C., Klebanov, P., et al. (2007). School readiness and later achievement. *Development Psychology, 43,* 1428–1446.

Dunn, L. M., & Dunn, D. M. (1997). *Peabody picture vocabulary test* (3rd ed.) (PPVT-III). Circle Pines, MN: American Guidance Service.

Ehri, L. (1996). Development of the ability to read words. In R. Barr, M. Kamil, P. B. Mosenthal, & P. D. Pearson (Eds.), *Handbook of reading research* (Vol. 2, pp. 383–418). Mahwah, NJ: Lawrence Erlbaum.

Ehri, L. C., & Roberts, T. (2006). The roots of learning to read and write: Acquisition of letters and phonemic awareness. In D. K. Dickinson & S. B. Neuman (Eds.), *Handbook of Early Literacy Research* (Vol. 2, pp. 113–131). New York: Guilford Press.

Every Child Ready to Read. (2005). *Storytime applications.* A Joint Project of the Public Library association and the Association for Library Service to Children. Retrieved April 3, 2009, from http://www.ala.org/ala/mgrps/divs/alsc/ecrr/ecrrinpractice/storytimeapplications/storytimeapplications.cfm

Frede, E. C. (1995). The role of program quality in producing early childhood program benefits. In R. E. Behrman (Ed.), *The future of children: Long-term outcomes of early childhood programs* (Vol. 5, pp. 115–132). Los Altos, CA: Center for the Future of Children.

References

Gilkerson, J., & Richards, J. A. (2008). *The power of talk.* Technical paper. Boulder, CO: Infoture, Inc. Retrieved April 3, 2009, from www.lenababy.com/TechReport.aspx/PowerOfTalk

Gillon, G. T. (2005). Facilitating phoneme awareness development in 3- and 4-year-old children with speech impairment. *Language, Speech, and Hearing Services in Schools, 36,* 308–324.

Gillon, G. T. (2004). *Phonological awareness: From research to practice.* New York: Guilford Press.

Goldsworthy, C. (1998, September). *Phonological awareness training: Where speech pathology meets reading.* Presentation at the National Scottish Rite Childhood Language Disorders Clinic and Learning Center Conference, "Linking Language and Literacy," Dallas, TX.

Gopnik, A., Meltzoff, A. N., & Kuhl, P. K. (1999). *The scientist in the crib: What early learning tells us about the mind.* New York: HarperCollins.

Hart, B., & Risley, T. R. (1995). *Meaningful differences in the everyday experiences of young children.* Baltimore: Paul H. Brookes.

Healy, J. (1999). *Failure to connect: How computers affect our children's minds—and what we can do about it.* New York: Touchstone Books.

International Reading Association (IRA) and the National Association for the Education of Young Children (NAEYC). (1998). Learning to read and write: Developmentally appropriate practices for young children. *Young Children, 93,* 30–46.

Justice, L. M. (2004, November/December). A team-based action plan for creating language-rich preschool classroom environments. *Council for Exceptional Children,* 2–10.

Kaderavek, J., & Sulzby, E. (1998). Parent-child joint book reading: An observational protocol for young children. *American Journal of Speech-Language Pathology, 7*(1), 33–47.

Landry, S. H., Anthony, J. A., Swank, P. R., Gunnewig, S., & Monseque-Bailey, P. (2007). *Effectiveness of comprehensive professional development for teachers of at-risk preschoolers.* Manuscript submitted for publication.

Landry, S. H., Crawford, A., Gunnewig, S., & Swank, P. R. (2002). *Teacher behavior rating scale.* Unpublished research instrument. Houston: Center for Improving the Readiness of Children for Learning and Education.

Landry, S. H., Swank, P. R., Smith, K. E., Assel, M. A., & Gunnewig, S. (2006). Enhancing early literacy skills for pre-school children: Bringing a professional development model to scale. *Journal of Learning Disabilities, 39,* 306–324.

Lonigan, C. J. (2006). Development, assessment, and promotion of preliteracy skills. *Early Education & Development, 17*(1), 91–114.

Lonigan, C. J., Burgess, S. R., & Anthony, J. L. (2000). Development of emergent literacy and early reading skills in preschool children: Evidence from a latent variable longitudinal study. *Developmental Psychology, 36,* 596–613.

Lonigan, C. J., Wagner, R. K., Torgesen, J. K., & Rashotte, C. A. (2007). *Test of preschool early literacy* (TOPEL). Austin, TX: ProEd.

Lyon, G. R., & Fletcher, J. (2001, Summer). Early warning system. *Education Matters 2001,* 23–29.

Machado, J. M. (1999). *Early childhood experiences in language arts* (6th ed.). Albany, NY: Delmar.

References

MacLean, M., Bryant, P., & Bradley, L. (1987). Rhymes, nursery rhymes, and reading in early childhood. *Merrill-Palmer Quarterly, 33,* 255–282.

McLaughlin, S. (1998). *Introduction to language development.* San Diego: Singular Publishing.

Metsala, J. L., & Walley, A. C. (1998). Spoken vocabulary growth and the segmental restructuring of lexical representations: Precursors to phoneme awareness and early reading ability. In J. L. Metsala & L. C. Ehri (Eds.), *Word recognition in beginning literacy* (pp. 89–120). Mahwah, NJ: Erlbaum.

Moats, L. C. (2009). *Language essentials for teachers of reading and spelling (LETRS®). Module 2—The speech sounds of English: Phonetics, phonology, and phoneme awareness* (2nd ed.). Longmont, CO: Sopris West Educational Services.

Moats, L. C. (2005/2006). How spelling supports reading: And why it is more regular and predictable than you may think. *American Educator,* 12–22.

Moats, L. C. (2005, January). *New perspectives on phonology and learning to read and spell.* LETRS (*Language Essentials for Teachers of Reading and Spelling*) Annual Meeting, Broomfield, CO.

Moats, L. C. (2000). *Speech to print: Language essentials for teachers.* Baltimore: Paul H. Brookes.

National Association for the Education of Young Children (NAEYC). (2009). Developmentally appropriate practice in early childhood programs serving children from birth through age 8. Available from NAEYC Web site: www.naeyc.org

National Association for the Education of Young Children (NAEYC). (1998). *Learning to read and write: Developmentally appropriate practices for young children.* A joint position statement of the International Reading Association and the National Association for the Education of Young Children. *Young Children, 53*(4), 30–46.

National Institute of Child Health and Human Development (NICHD). (2000). Report of the National Reading Panel. *Teaching children to read: Reports of the subgroups.* Washington, DC: National Institutes of Health. Retrieved April 3, 2009, from http://www.nichd.nih.gov/publications/nrp/report.cfm

National Institute for Literacy (NIFL). (2007, March). *Early literacy predictors of later reading outcomes.* Preliminary results from the National Early Literacy Panel. Louisville, KY: National Center for Family Literacy. Retrieved April 3, 2009, from http://www.nifl.gov/nifl/NELP_2007

National Reading Panel. (2000). *Teaching children to read: An evidence-based assessment of the scientific research literature on reading and its implications for reading instruction.* NIH Pub. No. 00-4769. Washington, DC: National Institute of Child Health and Human Development, National Institutes of Health. Retrieved April 3, 2009, from http://www.nichd.nih.gov/publications/nrp/smallbook.cfm

Neuman, S., Copple, C., & Bredekamp, S. (2000). *Learning to read and write: Developmentally appropriate practices for young children.* Washington, DC: National Association for the Education of Young Children.

Neuman, S. B., & Dickinson, D. K. (Eds.). (2002). *Handbook of early literacy research.* New York: Guilford Press.

Olsen, J. Z. (1998). *Handwriting without tears®: Kindergarten teacher's guide.* (7th rev. ed.). Cabin John, MD: Handwriting Without Tears.

References

Paulson, L. H. (2004). *The development of phonological awareness: From syllables to phonemes.* ProQuest Digital Dissertations.

Paulson, L. H., Noble, L. A., Jepson, S., & van den Pol, R. (2001). *Building early literacy and language skills* (BELLS). Longmont, CO: Sopris West Educational Services.

Paulson, L. H., & van den Pol, R. (1998). *Good talking words: A social communication skills program for young children.* Longmont, CO: Sopris West Educational Services.

Pinker, S. (1994). *The language instinct.* New York: HarperCollins.

Preschool Curriculum Evaluation Research Consortium. (2007). *Effects of preschool curriculum programs on school readiness.* National Center for Education Research, Institute of Education Sciences, U.S. Department of Education. Washington, DC: U.S. Government Printing Office.

Rvachew, S., Nowak, M., & Cloutier, G. (2004). Effect of phonetic perception training on the speech production and phonological awareness skills of children with expressive phonological delay. *American Journal of Speech-Language Pathology, 13*(3), 250–263.

Scarborough, H. S. (2002). Connecting early language and literacy to later reading (dis)abilities: Evidence, theory, and practice. In S. B. Neuman & D. K. Dickinson (Eds.), *Handbook of early literacy research* (pp. 97–110). New York: Guilford Press.

Scarborough, H. S. (1998). Early identification of children at risk for reading disabilities: Phonological awareness and some other promising predictors. In B. K. Shapiro, P. J. Accardo, & A. J. Capute (Eds.), *Specific reading disability: A view of the spectrum* (pp. 77–121). Timonium, MD: York Press.

Schickedanz, J. (1999). *Much more than the ABCs: The early stages of reading and writing.* Washington, DC: National Association for the Education of Young Children.

Schickedanz, J., & Casbergue, R. (2004). *Writing in preschool: Learning to orchestrate meaning and marks.* Newark, DE: International Reading Association.

Shaywitz, S. E. (2003). *Overcoming dyslexia: A new and complete science-based program for reading problems at any level.* New York: Knopf.

Snow, C. E., Burns, M. S., & Griffin, P. (Eds.). (1998). *Preventing reading difficulties in young children.* Washington, DC: National Academy Press.

Snowling, M., & Stackhouse, J. (1996). *Dyslexia speech and language: A practitioner's handbook.* San Diego: Singular Publishing Group.

Stanovich, K. E. (1992). Speculations on the causes and consequences of individual differences in early reading acquisition. In P. B. Gough, L. C. Ehri, & R. Treiman (Eds.), *Reading acquisition* (pp. 307–342). Hillsdale, NJ: Erlbaum.

Strickland, D. S. & Riley-Ayers, S. (2006). *Early literacy: Policy and practice in the preschool years.* National Institute for Early Education Research (NIEER) Policy Brief, Issue 10.

Sulzby, E. (1985). *Kindergarteners as writers and readers.* In M. Farr (Ed.), *Advances in writing research* (Vol. 1, pp. 127–199). Norwood, NJ: Ablex.

Torgesen, J. K. (2004, Fall). Preventing early reading failure—and its devastating downward spiral. *American Educator, 28,* 3.

Torgesen, J. K. (1999). Phonologically based reading disabilities. In R. J. Sternberg & L. Spear-Swerling (Eds.), *Perspectives of learning disabilities* (pp. 231–262). Boulder, CO: Westview Press.

References

Torgesen, J. K. (1998, Spring/Summer). Catch them before they fall: Identification and assessment to prevent reading failure in young children. *American Educator, 22,* 32–39.

van Kleeck, A. (1998). Preliteracy domains and stages: Laying the foundations for beginning reading. *Journal of Children's Communicative Development, 20*(1), 33–51.

Vukelich, C., & Christie, J. (2004). *Building a foundation for preschool literacy: Effective instruction for children's reading and writing development.* Newark, DE: International Reading Association.

Wagner, R. K., Torgesen, J. K., & Rashotte, C. A. (1994). Development of reading-related phonological processing abilities: New evidence of bidirectional causality from a latent variable longitudinal study. *Developmental Psychology, 30,* 73–87.

Whitehurst, G. J., Arnold, D. H., Epstein, J. N., Angell, A. L., Smith, M., & Fischel, J. E. (1994). A picture book reading intervention in day care and home for children from low-income families. *Developmental Psychology, 30,* 679–689.

Whitehurst, G. J., & Lonigan, C. J. (2002). Emergent literacy: Development from prereaders to readers. In S. B. Neuman & D. K. Dickinson (Eds.), *Handbook of early literacy research* (pp. 11–29). New York: Guilford Press.

Whitehurst, G. J., & Lonigan, C. J. (1998). Child development and emergent literacy. *Child Development, 69,* 848–872.

Wolfe, P., & Nevills, P. (2004). *Building the reading brain, PreK–3.* Thousand Oaks, CA: Corwin Press.

Zimmerman, I. L., Steiner, V. G., & Pond, R. E. (2002). *Preschool language scale* (4th ed) (PLS-4). San Antonio, TX: The Psychological Corporation.

Resources: LETRS® Supplementary Modules

(Modules are listed in sequential order.)

Moats, L. C. (2009a). *Language essentials for teachers of reading and spelling (LETRS) Module 1—The challenge of learning to read* (2nd ed.). Longmont, CO: Sopris West Educational Services.

Moats, L. C. (2009b). *Language essentials for teachers of reading and spelling (LETRS) Module 2—The speech sounds of English: Phonetics, phonology, and phoneme awareness* (2nd ed.). Longmont, CO: Sopris West Educational Services.

Moats, L. C. (2009c). *Language essentials for teachers of reading and spelling (LETRS) Module 3—Spellography for teachers: How English spelling works* (2nd ed.). Longmont, CO: Sopris West Educational Services.

Moats, L. C. (2009d). *Language essentials for teachers of reading and spelling (LETRS) Module 4—The mighty word: Building vocabulary and oral language* (2nd ed.). Longmont, CO: Sopris West Educational Services.

Moats, L. C. (2009e). *Language essentials for teachers of reading and spelling (LETRS) Module 5—Getting up to speed: Developing fluency* (2nd ed.). Longmont, CO: Sopris West Educational Services.

Moats, L. C. (2010a). *Language essentials for teachers of reading and spelling (LETRS) Module 6—Digging for meaning: Teaching text comprehension* (2nd ed.). Longmont, CO: Sopris West Educational Services.

Moats, L. C. (2010b). *Language essentials for teachers of reading and spelling (LETRS) Module 7—Teaching phonics, word study, and the alphabetic principle* (2nd ed.). Longmont, CO: Sopris West Educational Services.

Moats, L. C. (2005a). *Language essentials for teachers of reading and spelling (LETRS) Module 8—Assessment for prevention and early intervention (K–3)* (1st ed.). Longmont, CO: Sopris West Educational Services.

Moats, L. C. (2005b). *Language essentials for teachers of reading and spelling (LETRS) Module 9—Teaching beginning spelling and writing* (1st ed.). Longmont, CO: Sopris West Educational Services.

Moats, L. C. (2005c). *Language essentials for teachers of reading and spelling (LETRS) Module 10—Reading big words: Syllabication and advanced decoding* (1st ed.). Longmont, CO: Sopris West Educational Services.

Moats, L. C., & Sedita, J. (2006a). *Language essentials for teachers of reading and spelling (LETRS) Module 11—Writing: A road to reading comprehension* (1st ed.). Longmont, CO: Sopris West Educational Services.

Moats, L. C. (2006b). *Language essentials for teachers of reading and spelling (LETRS) Module 12—Using assessment to guide instruction (grade 3–adult)* (1st ed.). Longmont, CO: Sopris West Educational Services.

Appendix A
Preschool Curricula

Emerging Language and Literacy Curriculum (ELLC) (Sopris West® Educational Services, 2007)

The *Emerging Language and Literacy Curriculum* is an intentional, research-based early childhood curriculum with a strong emphasis on oral language and early literacy development. ELLC uses both implicit and explicit teaching strategies. All developmental domains are addressed through 22 storybook themes. Each unit focuses on a key concept with related vocabulary, language forms, a letter of the alphabet, and its speech sound. Eleven learning centers support each unit theme. Shared storybook-reading is an important component of ELLC and a time when children practice oral language skills. Phonological groups meet two times a week and focus on alliteration, onset-rimes, and segmenting and blending speech sounds. ELLC promotes a learning-rich environment that encourages adult-child interaction throughout the day. The program was used in a successful Early Reading First project in Missouri.

Building Language and Literacy (BLL) (Scholastic Inc., 2003)

BLL is a research-based program that develops children's oral language and early literacy skills, and can serve as the basis for an early literacy curriculum or can be integrated with a current one. Children are prepared for reading success with high-quality literature, songs, poems, vocabulary development, and language-loving characters. BLL is integrated with science, social studies, math, writing, music, and other curriculum and content areas. It provides targeted instruction that is followed with hands-on activities in oral language, phonological awareness, letter knowledge, and print knowledge. BLL includes built-in professional development and ongoing assessment.

Let's Begin with the Letter People (Abrams & Co., 2003)

Let's Begin with the Letter People is a comprehensive, thematically organized preschool program with a strong literacy and skills focus. Aligned with state and national pre-K standards, it includes a strong focus on skills development in print awareness, oral language and listening skills; phonological and phonemic awareness; alphabetic knowledge, including letter identification and sound-symbol association; vocabulary development; and early writing skills. Letter People are characters who come to life in the classroom and help engage children fully in early literacy activities. This program has been tested, with good results, in pilot studies by the University of Texas, Houston.

We Can!™: An Early Childhood Curriculum (Sopris West® Educational Services, 2003)

We Can! is a comprehensive early childhood curriculum that employs methods to promote reading and writing skills with thematic teaching, multisensory activities, and explicit instruction. Aligned with criteria in "Goals for Preschoolers" from the NAEYC and with the Head Start Path to Positive Child Outcomes, *We Can!* covers all the bases—language and literacy, math, science, social studies, fine arts, health/safety, personal/physical development, and even technology. One outstanding feature is the classroom management system that promotes student self-management, self-direction, and social growth within a system of clear routines and expectations.

Opening the World of Learning (OWL) (Pearson Education, 2005)

Research-based and field-tested, OWL is an integrated pre-K curriculum designed to develop language and early literacy skills in the context of rich content, primarily in the areas of mathematics, science, and social studies. Unit topics include Family, Friends, Wind and Water, World of Color, Shadows and Reflections, and Things That Grow.

Appendix B
Understanding Test Scores

(Based on material contributed by J. Ron Nelson, Ph.D.)

Key Concepts Necessary to Understand Scores

Screening, progress-monitoring, diagnostic, and outcome measures produce a variety of scores (i.e., numerical results produced by measures). Scores provide an efficient, effective, and objective way of characterizing the attribute or domain—called *constructs* in the measurement world—of interest. However, scores are tricky to understand. There are a number of concepts and issues that must be understood if scores are to be used effectively. In this section, we address some fundamental concepts necessary to understand scores.

Levels of Measurement

Understanding the measurement scale underlying a score is important to the interpretation of the numerical value(s) produced by a measure. The four levels of measurement, from lowest to highest level, include:

1. **Nominal**—Scores name an attribute or a domain.
2. **Ordinal**—Scores indicate a rank order within an attribute or a domain.
3. **Interval**—Scores indicate relative standing within a group, and also are based on an equal-interval scale.
4. **Ratio**—Scores describe relative or comparable amount of an attribute or a domain; includes an absolute zero.

Nominal measurement values simply "name" the attribute; no ordering or ranking of an attribute is provided. For example, a child's gender is a variable to which we can assign a value (e.g., 1 = female; 2 = male). A measurement value for gender simply represents a name. Because nominal values represent names, scores based on a nominal measurement scale are seldom, if at all, used to describe a child's performance or the quality of the preschool environment.

Ordinal measurement values "rank order," the attribute from better to worse or from worse to better; no information on the relative or comparable amount of an attribute is provided. In other words, these measurement values indicate more or less of the attribute, but not how much more or less. For example, children can be rank-ordered in terms of their height or weight (e.g., tallest to shortest; heaviest to lightest). The rank order of a specific group, such as a children in a classroom, does not tell us where any child is in relation to a national norm or a developmental norm. Because knowing the rank order of an attribute is relatively useful, scores based on an ordinal measurement scale are commonly used to describe a child's performance. Percentile ranks are a type of ordinal measurement.

Interval measurement values not only indicate rank order, but also the relative or comparable amount of an attribute. For example, on a standardized norm-referenced measure of phonological awareness, the interval or magnitude of the difference between standard score values is comparable. In this case, the interval between values is interpretable (e.g., the difference between 85 to 95 and 105 to 115 is the same). Because knowing the relative amount of an attribute is very useful, scores based on an interval measurement scale are commonly used to describe a child's performance. Such scores can also be used to compare a child's performance across measures or subtests within a measure, referred to as "intra-individual performance interpretation."

Ratio measurement values are similar to interval values in that they provide information on rank order and the relative or comparable amount of an attribute. However, ratio measurement scales have an absolute zero that is meaningful, but interval measurement scales have only a logical zero (e.g., a score of zero on an IQ test does not indicate the absence of intelligence). Weight is a score that is based on a ratio measurement scale. Because essentially all educational and psychological measures do not have an absolute zero, ratio measurement values are rarely, if at all, used in assessment.

It is important to recognize that there is a hierarchy implied in the level of measurement. At lower levels of measurement, numbers are less meaningful. At each level up the hierarchy, the current level includes all of the qualities of the one below it and adds something new. In general, it is desirable to have a higher level of measurement (e.g., interval) rather than a lower one (e.g., ordinal). Measures most frequently produce scores based on ordinal and interval measurement scales.

Types of Scores

Measures produce a range of different scores. As noted above, these scores are most often based on ordinal or interval levels of measurement. Thinking about the level of measurement or measurement scale provides a basic framework for understanding the type of information that a score provides. The different types of scores produced by measures include:
- raw scores
- criterion-referenced scores
- norm-referenced scores:
  — age and grade equivalents
  — percentile ranks
  — standard scores

Raw Scores

All measures produce a raw score. The raw score is typically the number of items answered correctly or observed, in the case of observational measures. Raw scores are typically converted because, in themselves, they are typically not meaningful. Thus, authors and publishers convert raw scores into the other scores that are described in the remainder of this section. The two major types of raw score transformations are *criterion-referenced* and *norm-referenced*. The transformations of both raw score types represent fundamentally different ways of describing the results from a measure.

Criterion-Referenced Scores

Criterion-referenced scores compare a child's performance (or other attribute) against an objective criterion or functional level of performance. The most common scores produced by criterion-referenced measures include "observed" or "not observed"; "occurred" or "not occurred"; "below basic," "basic," or "proficient," or some other variation on this theme. The scores are often expressed as percentages (e.g., the number of "observed" or "not observed" responses as a function of the total number of responses). Criterion-referenced scores are intuitive and easy to understand. Further, criterion-referenced scores are based on an ordinal measurement scale.

Norm-Referenced Scores

Norm-referenced scores compare a child's performance against a normative sample of children. Specific norm-referenced scores include the following types.

1. **Age- or grade-equivalent scores** describe the performance of a child in relation to the average performance of children in the normative group at the same age. For example, if a child receives an age-equivalent score of 3 years, 4 months (expressed as 3-4), on a measure of phonological awareness, the child performed the same as the average child at the 3rd year, 4th month, in the norm group. Grade scores are interpreted in a similar manner; for example, if a child receives a grade equivalent score of 1st grade, 2nd month (expressed as 1-2), the child's performance is the same as the average child in the 1st grade, 2nd month, in the norm group. Age- and grade-equivalent scores are based on an ordinal measurement scale.

2. **Percentile rank scores** indicate the rank of a child in comparison to 100 children of similar age or grade in the normative group. For example, if a child receives a percentile score of 55 (expressed as the 55th percentile), the child performed the same or better than 55% of the same age/grade children in the norm group. Inspection of *Figure B1* (next page) shows that the 50th percentile signifies average performance with the norm group. Percentile rank scores are based on an ordinal measurement scale.

3. **Standard scores** describe the performance of a child in relation to the average variability (standard deviation) of scores of the same age/grade children in the group. The normal distribution, or bell-shaped curve, plays a key role in interpreting standard scores from norm-referenced measures. In a normal distribution, 68% of scores of a typical group fall in the "average" range (i.e., within ±1 standard deviation of the mean). Scores between 1 and 2 standard deviations above and below the mean fall in the "above average" (an additional 14%) and "below average" (an additional 14%) range, respectively. Scores greater than 2 standard deviations above and below the mean fall in the "significantly above average" (approximately 2%) and "significantly below average"

(approximately 2%) range, respectively. The most widely used standard score scales are based on a scale where the average (mean) is 100 and the standard deviation is set at 15 points.

Stanines are another common standard score that have a mean of 5 and a standard deviation of 2. Stanines range from 1 to 9 and are an efficient way to communicate the range in which a child's score falls (e.g., "above average"). Other standard scores include the **t-score** (mean of 50 and standard deviation of 10), **z-score** (mean of 0 and standard deviation of 1), and **normal curve equivalents** (NCE; mean of 50 and standard deviation of 21.06). All standard scores are based on an interval measurement scale. Recall that interval level scores can be used to compare a child's performance across measures or subtests within a measure (referred to as *intra-individual performance interpretation*).

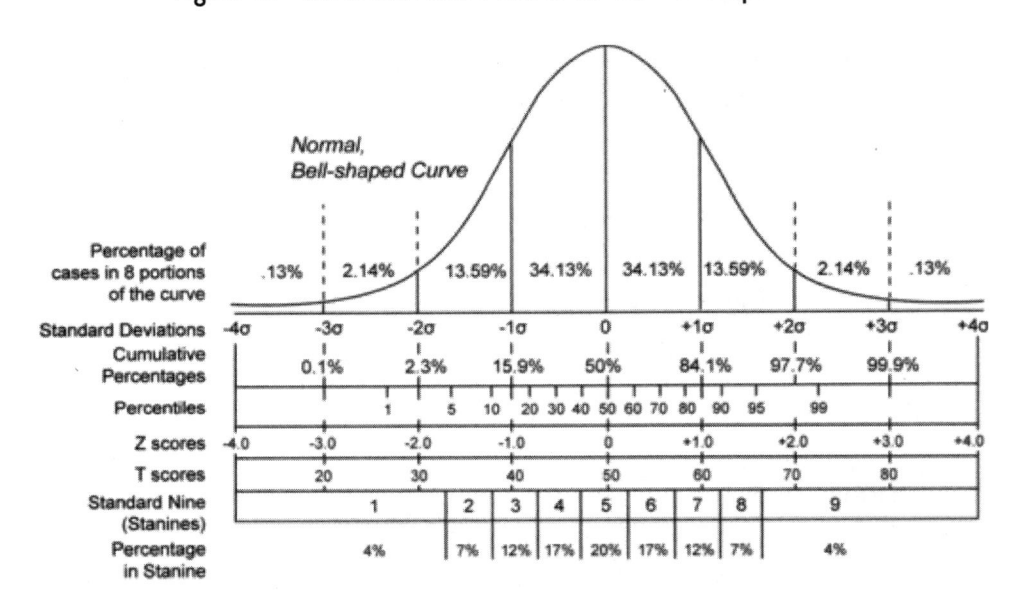

Figure B1 Norm-Referenced Scores on the Bell-Shaped Curve

Percentage of cases in 8 portions of the curve	.13% 2.14% 13.59% 34.13% 34.13% 13.59% 2.14% .13%
Standard Deviations	-4σ -3σ -2σ -1σ 0 +1σ +2σ +3σ +4σ
Cumulative Percentages	0.1% 2.3% 15.9% 50% 84.1% 97.7% 99.9%
Percentiles	1 5 10 20 30 40 50 60 70 80 90 95 99
Z scores	-4.0 -3.0 -2.0 -1.0 0 +1.0 +2.0 +3.0 +4.0
T scores	20 30 40 50 60 70 80
Standard Nine (Stanines)	1 2 3 4 5 6 7 8 9
Percentage in Stanine	4% 7% 12% 17% 20% 17% 12% 7% 4%

Scores Are Only Estimates

One of the most important concepts for the appropriate interpretation of scores is to understand that they are only *estimates* of the attribute or domain of interest (e.g., phonological awareness). This means that we can never know the true score or the exact magnitude of an attribute that lies within the person being assessed. The obtained or observed score comprises a true level of performance plus random error (see equation below). For example, we observe a child's performance on a measure of phonological awareness, which is reflected by the score (the left side of the equation). We are unable to observe the child's true performance and the amount of measurement error (the right side of the equation). In short, we should always keep in mind that scores produced by measures are only estimates of the unobservable "true score."

| Obtained/observed score | = | True Performance | + | Measurement error |

One of the strengths of norm-referenced measures is that the amount of measurement error is typically specified by a statistic called the *standard error of measurement* (i.e., SEM). The SEM can be used to establish 68% (± 1 SEM) and 95% (± 2 SEM) confidence intervals around an observed score. For example, in the case of a child who receives a standard score of 95 on a norm-referenced measure with an SEM of 4, our interpretations would be as follows:

- With 68% confidence, the child's true score falls between 91 and 99 (i.e., 95 ± 4).
- With 95% confidence, the child's true score falls between 87 and 103 (i.e., 95 ± 8).

The below 68% and 95% confidence interval interpretations demonstrate the importance of understanding that score or values produced by a measure are only estimates of an attribute. Unfortunately, many measures (e.g., observation rating scales) used with young children are not norm-referenced and do not provide an index of measurement error (i.e., SEM). In these cases, there are three possible solutions:

1. *Interpret the scores or values produced by a measure very cautiously.* The degree of caution should increase as the score deviates from average because errors of measurement increase as scores deviate from average or typical. There is little doubt that measures that have not gone through rigorous psychometric studies to establish their reliability and validity are prone to large errors of measurement.
2. *Use multiple measures of the same attribute.* The scores from the different measures can be triangulated to get a more accurate sense of the child's performance.
3. *Assess the attribute of interest multiple times.* Typically, the median score from three measurement sessions will provide a relatively accurate sense of the child's performance.

Finally, using the SEM and associated confidence intervals allows one to assess strengths and weaknesses in a child's performance across tests or subtest within a test. This is commonly referred to as an *intra-individual performance interpretation* and is restricted to scores based on an interval measurement scale. For example, the standard scores (based on a mean of 100 and standard deviation of 15) and associated 68% confidence intervals (SEM = ± 4) for two different children on an alphabet knowledge and phonological awareness are presented in *Table B1* (next page). In the case of Allie, inspection of the 68% confidence intervals reveals differences in her alphabet knowledge and phonological awareness (i.e., the confidence intervals do not overlap with one another). Allie shows strength in phonological awareness relative to alphabet knowledge. In the case of Jorge, inspection of the 68% confidence intervals reveals no differences in his alphabet knowledge and phonological awareness (i.e., confidence intervals overlap with one another). Jorge does not show a relative strength or weakness in alphabet knowledge and phonological awareness. Finally, although some measures provide specific guidelines for making intra-individual performance interpretations, the 68% or 95% confidence intervals can be used to establish relative strengths and weaknesses in those cases when guidelines are not provided.

Appendix B

Table B1 Comparison of Two Children's Test Scores

Child	Subtest	Standard Score	68% Confidence Interval
Allie	• Alphabet knowledge	80	76–84
	• Phonological awareness	92	88–96
Jorge	• Alphabet knowledge	82	78–86
	• Phonological awareness	85	81–89

Reliability

The SEM provides an indication of the technical quality of a measure and is based on and related directly to *reliability*. As the reliability of a measure increases, its SEM decreases, and vice versa. Reliability refers to the "consistency" or "repeatability" of measures or observations. A test must be reliable to be valid. A valid test measures what its authors and publishers claim the test measures. In other words, reliability is a necessary condition—but not the only condition—that must be met for a test to be valid. Although it is not possible to establish the reliability of a measure exactly, four approaches are used to estimate the reliability of a measure:

1. **Test-retest reliability** estimates the consistency of the results of the same measure administered to the same sample on two different occasions (typically, two to four weeks apart).
2. **Parallel-forms reliability** estimates the consistency of the results of two or more forms of the same measure administered to the same sample at the same time.
3. **Internal consistency reliability** estimates the consistency of results across items within the same measure administered to the same sample at the same time.
4. **Inter-rater, or inter-observer, reliability** estimates the extent to which different raters/observers give consistent estimates of an attribute on the same sample at the same time.

These four approaches to reliability provide different estimates of reliability. *Test-retest reliability* provides one of the most important estimates of the consistency of a measure over time. Most attributes (e.g., phonological awareness) change slowly over a short period of time. Radical and unpredictable changes in children's scores on a phonological awareness over a short period of time would raise concerns about the reliability of a measure. *Parallel-forms reliability* is important for measures in which you intend to use alternative forms. For example, you would use one form of measure in the beginning of the school year and another form at the end of the school year to measure growth in children's phonological awareness. *Internal consistency reliability* is important for measures that include multiple items that measure the same attribute (e.g., 10-item rating scale of phonological awareness). In effect, the reliability of a measure is judged by estimating how well the items that reflect the same attribute yield similar results. *Inter-rater*, or *inter-observer, reliability* is important in those cases in which observations are being conducted. One's confidence in the results is enhanced when two raters rate a child's phonological awareness in a similar fashion. Finally, keep in mind that each of these approaches to reliability will yield a different estimate of reliability. In general, test-retest reliability estimates are lower in value than parallel-forms, internal consistency, and inter-rater/inter-observer reliability estimates.

It is important to consider the reliability factor when using a measure. Ideally, test authors and publishers should present reliability estimates for any scale or subscale scores that are to be interpreted. For example, if a measure of phonological awareness includes rhyming, alliteration, and phonemic awareness subscales, reliability estimates should be presented for each. It is especially useful (and recommended) that authors and publishers provide information on the SEM to aid in the interpretation of scores.

The reliability coefficient is the most widely reported statistic for expressing the reliability of a measure. Reliability coefficient values range from 0 (absence of reliability) to 1.00 (perfect reliability). One way of viewing reliability coefficients is to think about them as indicators of the accuracy of a score. You begin by squaring the reliability coefficient (i.e., called the *coefficient of determination*) to provide an index of true variability or explained variance. A squared reliability coefficient of .90 s indicates that 81% of the variability of a score is true variability or explained variance and 19% consists of error variance that is unexplained. Note that small changes in reliability coefficients result in large changes in the amount of true variability (see *Table B2*). Finally, reliability coefficients for screening and progress-monitoring measures generally do not need to be as high as those of diagnostic and outcome measures. Screening results lead to the use of an intervention and/or further assessment, and progress monitoring involves repeated measurement of the same child over time. One should expect large reliability coefficients (i.e., ≥ 90) in the case of diagnostic and outcome measures (Salvia, Ysseldyke, & Bolt, 2007).

Table B2 Reliability and Explained Variance

Reliability Coefficient	Coefficient of Determination	Explained Variance	Error Variance
.90	.81	81%	19%
.80	.64	64%	36%
.70	.49	49%	51%
.60	.36	36%	64%
.50	.25	25%	75%

Validity

Validity is considered to be the most important technical characteristic of a measure; all other characteristics of a measure (e.g., reliability) are subsumed under validity. Validity addresses the extent to which the measure assesses what it is designed to measure. As with reliability, it is not possible to establish the validity of a measure exactly. The five approaches used to estimate the validity of a measure are as follows:

1. **Face validity** refers to a nontechnical review of a measure to determine whether it appears valid on the surface. Face validity is estimated subjectively by simply reviewing the items on a measure to see if they appear to measure an attribute or domain.
2. **Content validity** refers to the extent to which a measure covers the attribute or domain of interest. Content validity is estimated via a formal analysis of the content of a measure by the authors or other professionals.
3. **Concurrent validity** refers to the extent to which the results of a measure are consistent with those of another valid measure of the same attribute or domain. Concurrent validity is estimated by correlating the results from a measure with another valid measure of the same attribute that is administered to the same sample at the same time (e.g., two preschool phonological awareness measures are correlated with one another).
4. **Predictive validity** refers to how well a measure predicts an important attribute or outcome in the future. Predictive validity is estimated by correlating the results from a measure with another valid measure of an important related attribute that is administered to the same sample at two different points in time (e.g., a preschool phonological awareness measure is correlated with a kindergarten readiness measure).
5. **Construct validity** refers to how well a measure assesses a theoretical construct. Construct validity is estimated through multiples studies of the inter-correlations between and among measures.

The five approaches to validity provide different estimates of validity. *Face* and *content validity* provide subjective qualitative information regarding the validity of a measure. *Concurrent validity* provides one of the most important estimates of the validity of a measure. Radical and unpredictable differences in children's scores on a phonological awareness measure from an established valid measure of phonological awareness would raise concerns about the validity of a measure. *Predictive validity* is important for measures in which you would like to predict an attribute or outcome in the future. *Construct validity* is the highest form of validity, and it takes a great deal of time and multiple studies to fully establish.

It is important to consider the validity factor when using a measure. The validity coefficient is the most widely reported statistic for expressing the validity of a measure. Similar to reliability coefficients, validity coefficient values range from 0 (absence of validity) to 1.00 (perfect validity). It is important to note that validity coefficients typically are smaller than reliability coefficients. Ideally, test authors and publishers should present validity estimates for any scale or subscale scores that are to be interpreted. Because the validity of a measure is the combined responsibility of the measure's author and publisher and the user of the measure, a great deal of caution should be used when using measures. Several factors related directly to the user of a measure (e.g., administration and scoring errors) have an adverse effect on the validity of a test.

Reference

Salvia, J., Ysseldyke, J. E., & Bolt, S. (2007). *Assessment in special and inclusive education* (10th ed.). Boston: Houghton Mifflin.

Appendix C
Developing Preschool Measures

(Based on material contributed by J. Ron Nelson, Ph.D.)

Fundamental Principles Underlying Screening and Progress-Monitoring Measures

Screening and progress monitoring of young children's early literacy and language growth is critical to the success of all children. Unfortunately, in contrast to the well-developed curriculum-based measurement (CBM) screening and progress-monitoring probes in reading, mathematics, and written language, there are few well-established CBM probes available to assess young children's early literacy and language growth (e.g., *Get It, Got It, Go!* Individual Growth and Development Indicators; McConnell, Priest, Davis, & McEvoy, 2002). Before going on, it is important to note that there are well-established CBM screening and progress-monitoring tools for children's early numeracy (e.g., see Web sites http://www.interventioncentral.org or http://www.aimsweb.com). Further, few screening and progress-monitoring measures have clear benchmark criteria with which to compare a child's performance to a well-defined normative group. However, teachers working with young children may be able to use some less established screening and progress-monitoring measures if they follow the fundamental principles underlying established CBM probes and interpret the data cautiously (see "Key Concepts Necessary to Understand Scores" in *Appendix B*). The steps that involve application of those principles are:

1. Creation of measures.
2. Development of standardized administration procedures.
3. Creation of local benchmarks.
4. Use of graphing and instructional decision rules.

Create Measures

CBM screening and progress-monitoring measures can be created or identified among the assessment tools used in conjunction with curriculum programs or even other measures/observation frameworks. The goal is to identify a set of objective stimulus materials or observation frameworks that relate to the early literacy and language skills being taught. The stimulus materials or observation frameworks can be secured by soliciting information and feedback from a variety of classroom teachers and validating them by examining the curriculum materials, embedded program assessments, and instructional scope and sequence. It is important to avoid developing screening and progress-monitoring assessments with "floor and ceiling" effects; that is, the measure should be easy enough for all children to succeed on some items and hard enough so that no child gets all the items correct. Finally, it is important to keep in mind that screening and progress-monitoring procedures should be brief and easy to implement.

Develop Standardized Administration Procedures

Standardized administration procedures are necessary to obtain accurate screening and progress-monitoring data. Standardized administration typically includes procedures to ensure:

- that children understand the task or requirement;
- the timing or length of the assessment period;
- neutral interaction with children during the assessment period (e.g., feedback for correct and incorrect responses should not influence children's responses); and
- standardized scoring procedures.

Although some of these procedures may not apply to certain measures (e.g., observations), it is critical that the performance (screening) of each child occurs under the same conditions and procedures each time (progress monitoring). If identical conditions and procedures are not used, screening and progress-monitoring scores will differ because a child's performance may have been a function of a change in the procedures rather than actual growth.

Create Local Benchmarks

The effective implementation and use of screening and progress-monitoring assessments do not require large normative samples. Local norms (i.e., classroom and program levels) can be developed quite easily and efficiently. Two methods can be used to establish local benchmarks:

- Obtain a random subsample from the classroom or the program, or
- Obtain a sample from "typical" children (i.e., children with average early literacy and language skills).

Although there is no set standard regarding the number of children necessary to establish accurate local benchmarks, available research on the adequacy of sample size suggests that five to ten randomly selected children is sufficient (Tindal, Germann, & Deno, 1983). Of course, benchmarks can be updated on a regular basis using the actual screening and progress-monitoring data that is collected over time. A simple Excel® file or other database system can be used to enter, store, and analyze the data. Finally, local benchmarks should be established on a trimester (i.e., three times per year) basis to reflect children's growth.

Use Graphing and Instructional Decision Rules

The purpose of progress monitoring is to document change in child performance over time to determine whether children are progressing appropriately in a particular instructional program. Graphing data is the typical process used to document change in child performance over time. Visual display of the information aids interpretation of the results. In this way, the results of effective (see *Figure C1*, p. 140) or ineffective (see *Figure C2*, p. 141) instructional programs or interventions can be demonstrated visually across time. Teachers can use standard graphing paper or download graphing forms or automated progress-monitoring charts from the Web site http://www.interventioncentral.org/htmdocs/

interventions/cbmwarehouse.php. Teachers then apply instructional decision-making rules to the graphed data to determine if and when an instructional change is warranted. When warranted, teachers can use the following instructional decision-making rules to monitor child progress and to make changes in instruction and interventions (review *Figures C1* and *C2* in conjunction with these descriptions of instructional decision-making rules):

1. Collect baseline performance (typically the median of three data points), and set an end-of-year performance goal or benchmark. Indicate baseline data with a dotted line. Connect baseline performance to the goal to show the goal line or students' anticipated rate of progress through the year or instructional timeframe to meet the goal. The goal line provides an index with which to gauge the extent to which students' rate of progress is adequate to meet the established goal.

2. Draw a dotted vertical line following the last baseline point to indicate the beginning of an instruction and interventions phase. Continue to monitor student performance on a frequent basis (i.e., one to two times per week). Graph the scores to allow for ongoing ocular analysis of students' rate of growth relative to the goal line.

3. Employ the Four-Point Rule: After three to six weeks of implementing a change in instruction and interventions (at least six data points must be collected), examine the most recent four data points. If all four consecutive data points fall above the goal line, consider raising the goal. If the goal is changed, draw another dotted vertical line and reestablish a new goal line. If all four consecutive data points fall below the goal line, draw a solid vertical line and implement a change in instruction and interventions.

4. Employ the Trend Rule: In cases in which four consecutive data points fall both above and below the goal line, keep collecting data. After collecting at least eight data points, a trend line can be drawn that represents a line of best fit through the data. This trend line shows the relative rate of progress students are making during the most recent instructional phase. Compare the trend line to the goal line. If the trend line is steeper than the goal line, draw a dotted vertical line and raise the goal. If the trend line is less steep than the goal line, draw a solid vertical line and implement a change in instruction and interventions. It is important to note that the Four-Point Rule (description #3, above) supersedes the Trend Rule.

5. If either the Four-Point Rule or the Trend Rule indicates that students are not progressing at the anticipated rate, a change in instruction and interventions should be made. The educator may be implementing instruction and interventions that are working well for other students but are not working well for a particular student. The educator attempts to match the instruction and interventions to the needs of students who are not progressing as anticipated. The educator may vary the:
   - type or content of instruction;
   - instructional intensity in terms of opportunities for students to respond;
   - allocated time for instruction;

- curriculum materials used; or
- motivational strategies incorporated during instruction.

After the educator determines the nature of change in instruction and interventions, the new plan should be implemented for a minimum of three weeks prior to applying CBM decision-making rules to determine the success of the instruction and interventions.

6. Continue collecting CBM data on a frequent basis, and apply these standard decision-making rules for each phase of instruction.

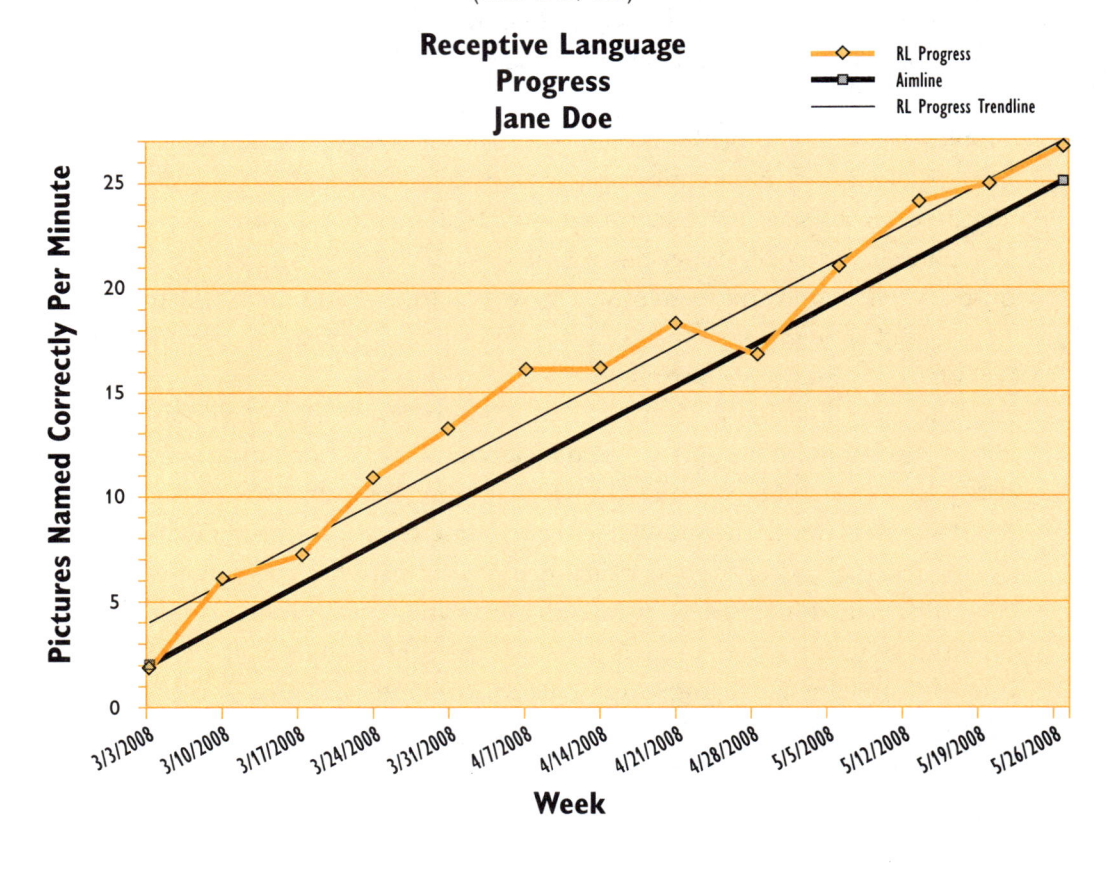

Figure C1 Example of a Progress-Monitoring Graph When a Child Is Responding to the Instructional Program or Intervention

(Tindal et al., 1983)

Figure C2 Example of a Progress-Monitoring Graph When a Child Is not Responding to the Instructional Program or Intervention

(Tindal et al., 1983)

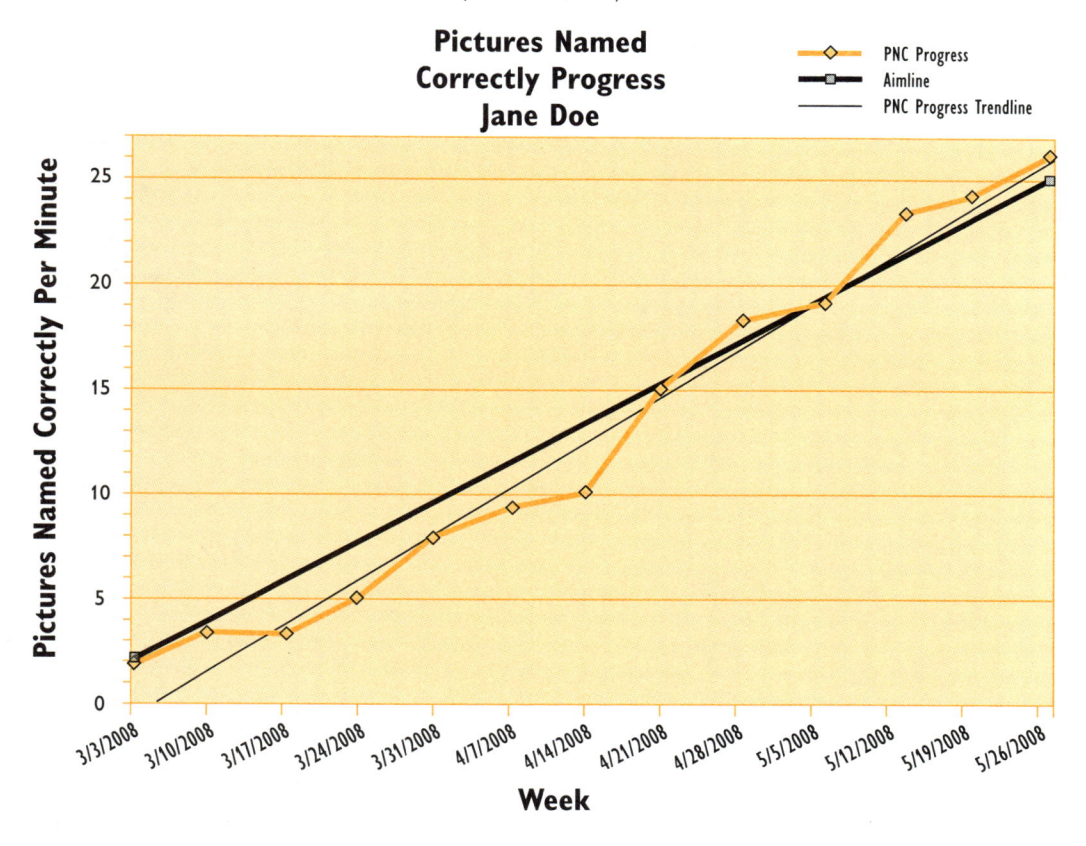

Pictures Named Correctly Progress Jane Doe

References

McConnell, S. R., Priest, J. S., Davis, S. D., & McEvoy, M. (2002). Best practices in measuring growth and development for preschool children. In A. Thomas & J. Grimes (Eds.), *Best practices in school psychology IV* (pp. 1231–1246). Bethesda, MD: NASP.

Tindal, G., Germann, G., & Deno, S. L. (1983). *Descriptive research on the Pine County norms: A compilation of findings* (Research Rep. No. 132). Minneapolis: University of Minnesota Institute for Research on Learning Disabilities.

Answer Key

Chapter 1
Early Literacy Connections

Exercise 1.1: Environmental Supports (p. 6)
- List all literacy opportunities you can think of that are typically found in a preschool environment.

Lists should include:
- the presence of books and print material
- the routine of story time
- the presence of signs and labels on objects
- posters and wall charts of the alphabet and important vocabulary words
- the presence of coloring and tracing books, etc.

Exercise 1.2: Foundations for the Essential Components (p. 8)
- What early literacy foundation area is necessary for each reading and writing component?

Early Literacy Area	Reading/Writing Component
Phonological awareness	Phonemic awareness
Phonological awareness, print knowledge	Phonics
Oral language, phonological awareness	Vocabulary
Oral language, phonological awareness	Fluency
Oral language	Comprehension
Print knowledge, phonological awareness	Spelling
Print knowledge, phonological awareness, oral language	Writing

Answer Key

Exercise 1.3: How the Phonological Processing System Works (p. 11)

— Say aloud the word for the largest member of the feline family that has orange and black stripes.

— Then, say the word without the /g/ sound.

— You said **tiger**, and then fairly easily deducted the word **tire**.

- What phonological processing skills were required for you to complete this task?

During this process, you needed to retain the word tiger in your phonological memory, manipulate the sounds using your phonological awareness skills, and then come up with a different word using your phonological retrieval or naming skills.

Exercise 1.4: A Young Child's Phonological Production (p. 13)

1. What was this child's phonological representation for this animal?
   His phonological representation for this animal was "hippo."

2. Describe how this child used each of these elements of phonological processing:
   Phonological memory **He held the word hippopotamus in his phonological memory.**

   Phonological awareness **He used phonological awareness skills to manipulate the word by adding more syllables.**

   Phonological naming **He retrieved a new word.**

Exercise 1.5: Phonological Processor vs. Orthographic Processor (p. 14)

- What is this story about? **"Little Red Riding Hood"**
- How far did you have to read before you knew what the story was about?
  (Answers will vary.)

Exercise 1.6: Rate Your Current Beliefs (p. 16)

(Answers will vary.)

Chapter 2
The Oral Language Connection to Literacy

Exercise 2.1: Singing With Vowels and Consonants (p. 23)
- Sing the alphabet song saying only the vowel sounds in the syllable; for example, sing, "ā, ē, ē, ē" for "a, b, c, d." (Be careful to not "close" your mouth with your tongue or jaw.) Listen to the vowel sounds you are singing. What vowel sounds do you hear the most?
  Long a (/ā/) and long e (/ē/).
- Now sing the song again, this time with only the consonant sounds in the syllables; for example, sing, "___, /b/, /s/, /d/" for "a, b, c, d."
- Which version was easier to understand: the vowel or the consonant version?
  The vowel version, because vowel sounds are more like speech. Consonant sounds are more distinctive, although they are more difficult to say in isolation and do not make syllables (because there are no vowel sounds!).

Exercise 2.2: Evaluate Consonant Sounds (p. 23)
- Which consonant sounds are most perceptible?
  Consonant sounds made in the front of the mouth are the most perceptible because, when considering placement, you can "see" them being produced.

Exercise 2.3: Select a Sound for Instruction (p. 24)
Identifying the /s/ sound in the word sun. Sounds that can be said for a longer period of time give a child a better chance to perceive the presence of the sound; /s/ is easier to perceive than /t/.

Exercise 2.4: Consonant Sounds With Voicing (p. 25)
- Which consonant sounds must be pronounced with voicing or vocalization?
  The voiced stop sounds—/b/, /d/, /g/, /j/—are pronounced with a vowel sound, making it harder for a young child to isolate the consonant sound from the attending vowel sound. Young children will often segment a word such as bug into two sounds—/bŭ/ /g/—because when saying /b/, they also hear the attending vowel sound.

Answer Key

Exercise 2.5: Phonemic Awareness: Count the Phonemes (p. 26)

Word	Identity of sounds	Number of sounds
string	/s/ /t/ /r/ /ĭ/ /ng/	5
joyless	/j/ /oi/ /l/ /ə/ /s/	5
dodge	/d/ /ŏ/ /j/	3
mixed	/m/ /ĭ/ /k/ /s/ /t/	5
heard	/h/ /er/ /d/	3
crash	/k/ /r/ /ă/ /sh/	4
though	/th/ /ō/	2
chew	/ch/ /ū/	2
house	/h/ /ou/ /s/	3
quiet	/k/ /w/ /ī/ /ə/ /t/	5

Exercise 2.6: List Vocabulary Words in a Storybook (p. 28)
(Answers will vary.)

Exercise 2.7: Add Morphological Endings (p. 29)

Morpheme	Part of speech
-s	**talks** (plural noun or third person progressive verb)
-er	**talker** (descriptive noun)
-ed	**talked** (past tense verb)
-ing	**talking** (present progressive verb)
-ative	**talkative** (adjective)
-tion	**talktion** (doesn't work!)

Exercise 2.8: Divide Words by Syllables and Morphemes (p. 30)

Word	Syllable division	Morpheme division
reader	rea-der	read-er
hats	hats	hat-s
rented	ren-ted	rent-ed
underplayed	un-der-played	under-play-ed
kangaroo	kan-ga-roo	kangaroo
biography	bi-o-gra-phy	bio-graph-y

Exercise 2.9: Locate Morphemes (p. 31)
(Answers will vary.)

Exercise 2.10: Quantify Sentence Length (p. 32)
(Answers will vary.)

Exercise 2.11: Experiment With Prosodic Stress (p. 33)

1. She got a pink slip.
   She got a notice of job termination; or
   She bought some underwear.

2. I saw a man eating shark.
   I saw a man who was eating shark; or
   I saw a man-eating shark.

3. She fed her dog bones.
   She fed dog bones to her (another female dog or a female visitor); or
   She fed bones to her dog; or
   She fed her dog named Bones.

Exercise 2.12: A Case Study (p. 39)
(Answers are embedded in the exercise.)

Answer Key

Exercise 2.13: Expand Utterances (p. 41)

Examples of sentence expansion:
1. It's a big ball.
2. The dog ate the bone.
3. That's right, she fell down the hill.
4. Yes, he blew a gigantic bubble.

Exercise 2.14: Match the Type of Response to the Sentence (p. 42)

a. Waiting	d	1. A child says, "I made a snake!" and the teacher responds, "Yes, you made a snake."
b. Extending	b	2. A child says, "Look, I made a snake," and the teacher replies, "You made a long blue and green snake."
c. Pausing	e	3. A child says, "Look, I made a snake," and the teacher replies, "You made a snake."
d. Confirming	a	4. The teacher rolls out her play dough while watching the children and then comments, "I like rolling out play dough."
e. Imitating	c	5. After using a tree-shaped cookie cutter, the teacher says, "Look, I made a yellow ... " and waits for a response.
f. Labeling	f	6. A child chooses a cookie cutter and the teacher says, "You are going to make a red triangle."
g. Scripting	g	7. A child chooses a cookie cutter and the teacher says, "You are making a red triangle. Tell me what you are making."

Exercise 2.15: Practice Language Modeling (p. 43)

Scenario 2: During a book-reading activity looking at big trucks and moving machines, a child points to a bulldozer but does not label it.		
"I Do It"	You say, "It's a bulldozer. Let's say it together."	
"We Do It"	You and the child say, "Bulldozer."	
"You Do It"	You say, "Now you say it." The child should respond, "Bulldozer."	
Scenario 3: At a tabletop activity glueing shapes onto a piece of paper, one child grabs the glue from another child who, in turn, hits the grabber. What techniques would you use for the grabber and the hitter?		
"I Do It"	*Grabber:* To the grabber, you say, "You need some glue. Let's tell Josiah, 'I need glue, please.'" *Hitter:* To the hitter, you say, "Tell Sarah, 'I have the glue.' Now you try it."	
"We Do It"	*Grabber:* Both you and the grabber say, "I need glue, please." Then you say, "Nice, now it's your turn." *Hitter:* Both you and the hitter say, "I have the glue." Then you say, "Now it's your turn."	
"You Do It"	*Grabber:* The grabber says to the hitter, "I need glue, please." *Hitter:* The hitter says, "I have the glue."	

In these situations, you always have to decide what to address and what to ignore. However, these quick verbal exchanges provide a teachable moment for the direct instruction children need to learn social interaction skills, and these kinds of exchanges are much more productive than "No hitting!" or "Share the glue."

Answer Key

Exercise 2.16: Practice Scaffolding (p. 45)
(Answers will vary.)

Exercise 2.17: Identify the Hierarchy of Questions (p. 46)

	Hierarchy Level
1. Which one is bigger, the dog or the cat?	Analysis
2. Who is on the slumbering mouse?	Recall
3. What is the weather like?	Synthesis
4. What happened when the flea bit the mouse?	Application
5. Why did the flea bite the mouse?	Evaluation

Reflection and Review (p. 48)

1. Describe the five structures of oral language.
   - **phonology**: the study of the speech sounds of a language and the rules that are used to put them together to form words
   - **semantics**: the study of word and phrase meanings
   - **morphology**: the rules of word formation
   - **syntax**: the grammatical rules that govern word order in sentences
   - **prosody**: the rhythm and intonation aspect of spoken language

2. List the stages of oral language and literacy development and the characteristics of each stage.
   - **Stage 1** (before symbolic relationships are established)
     Oral language: prelexic; Written language: prelogographic
   - **Stage 2** (simple whole-word and print representations)
     Oral language: lexic; Written language: logographic (prealphabetic)
   - **Stage 3** (simplifications of language structures)
     Oral language: systematic simplification; Written language: early alphabetic
   - **Stage 4** (developing awareness of the structures of language)
     Oral language: assembly; Written language: later alphabetic
   - **Stage 5** (ability to manipulate language structures)
     Oral language: metaphonological; Written language: consolidated alphabetic

3. Describe language facilitation, scaffolding, and dialogic reading, and how these techniques are used with children.
   Language facilitation: **Techniques used by adults to foster children's oral language and vocabulary development. Techniques include:**

- Parallel talk, self-talk, and expansion, which provide children with models of simple to complex language.
- Child-oriented responses that focus on the child to maintain a conversation.
- Interaction responses that encourage children to talk.
- Language-modeling to demonstrate word meaning, structure, and how language is used.

Scaffolding: Techniques used by adults to encourage children to perform at progressively higher language levels.

Dialogic reading: Shared storybook-reading to help children develop vocabulary, expand their language, and learn more about how print works.

4. How does knowing about the structures of oral language help us teach young children?
Understanding more about the structures of oral language helps us to identify what children are able to do and to determine what they need to learn.

Chapter 3
Phonological Awareness Connections

Exercise 3.1: Phonological or Phonemic Awareness? (p. 52)

- The teacher asks, "What's this word: *e-le-phant*. The children answer, "Elephant."
  — Is this an example of phonological awareness? Phonemic awareness?
  Phonological awareness

- While taking attendance, the teacher asks, "Who's here? K-K-Katy, Sh-Sh-ane ... ?"
  — Is this an example of phonological awareness? Phonemic awareness?
  Both

Exercise 3.2: List Rhyming Words (p. 55)
Example answers: **Jill, hill; down, crown; dock, clock**

Exercise 3.3: Generate Rhyming Words (p. 56)
Examples of words that rhyme with **cat**:
bat, fat, drat, gnat, hat, mat, sat, rat, slat, vat
Examples of words that rhyme with **chef**:
clef, Jeff, ref

Answer Key

Exercise 3.4: Isolate Initial Sounds (p. 58)

sun /s/	write /r/	fish /f/	cup /k/	zipper /z/
sugar /sh/	white /w/	phone /f/	cent /s/	xylophone /z/
shoe /sh/	ring /r/	pole /p/	chair /ch/	
			Chris /k/	

Exercise 3.5: Determine the Level of Linguistic Analysis (p. 60)

- What is the linguistic level of each example: *syllable*, *onset-rime*, or *phoneme*?

1. A teacher says, "I see a **kan-ga-roo**!" and children reply, "Kangaroo!"
   Syllable

2. A teacher says, "I want to see **T-asha**," and Tasha comes over.
   Onset-rime

3. A teacher says, "I want a block that is **r-e-d**," and a child provides a red block.
   Phoneme

Exercise 3.6: Identify Syllables and Phonemes (p. 61)

- Answers will vary. Example answers:
  horse (1); elephant (3); rhinoceros (4); camel (2); hippopotamus (5)
- Answers will vary. Example answers:
  tiger-toucan; hummingbird-hippo; gazelle-goose; giraffe-junco; kangaroo-camel
- Answers will vary. Example answers:
  cow, /k/ /ow/ (2); **horse,** /h/ /or/ /s/ (3); **dog,** /d/ /ŏ/ /g/ (3); **duck,** /d/ /ŭ/ /k/ (3); **pig,** /p/ /ĭ/ /g/ (3)

Reflection and Review (p. 67)

1. What are the four components of phonological awareness?
   Rhyming, alliteration, blending, and segmenting.

2. List the developmental sequences of each component of phonological awareness.
   Rhyming:
   - **Say words in songs and fingerplays.**
   - **Match words that rhyme.**
   - **Produce words that rhyme.**

Alliteration:
- **Match words that begin with the same sound.**
- **Produce words that begin with the same sound.**

Blending:
- **Blend words from syllables**
- **Blend words from onset-rime**
- **Blend words from separate phonemes.**

Segmenting:
- **Pull apart words into syllables.**
- **Pull apart words into onset-rime.**
- **Pull apart words into phonemes.**

3. What strategies can be used to build phonological awareness in young children?
   Both formal and informal strategies can be used:
   Rhyme:
   - **Sing songs, use lots of word play, read rhyme books, play rhyme games (e.g., rhyme activities in BELLS [Paulson et al., 2001]).**

   Blending and segmenting:
   - **Use lots of word play, play guessing games using word structures (e.g., activities in BELLS [Paulson et al., 2001]).**

Chapter 4
Written Language Connections

Exercise 4.1: Inform Instruction About Print Concepts (p. 74)
- List three ways you can help children develop their concepts of print in each of these areas:

1. Recognizing print in our surroundings:
   Answers will vary. Example answers:
   - **Post a large calendar so that children can clearly see the names of months and days of the week.**
   - **Print children's names in their cubbies.**
   - **Look for occurrences of the letter B when reading the book** *Brown Bear, Brown Bear, What Do You See?*

2. Understanding that print carries meaning:
   Answers will vary. Example answers:
   - **Choose song cards for favorite songs to sing.**
   - **Use icons to represent different Center Activities.**
   - **Find a favorite book.**

3. Knowing that print is used for many purposes:
   Answers will vary. Example answers:
   - **Print is found all around us in books and magazines; on signs, food containers, and clothes; for directions, such as recipes; for lists and writing directions; on mail and notes; on computers, televisions, and videos; on puzzles, letters, blocks, and electronic toys that highlight letters and numbers.**

4. Experiencing print through writing:
   Answers will vary. Example answers:
   - **Have children sign their names on a sign-up sheet as they arrive.**
   - **Fill in a feeding chart for the class pet turtle.**
   - **Make street signs for a pretend road scene in the building-block area.**

Exercise 4.2: Make Letter Forms (p. 79)
(Answers will vary.)

Answer Key

Exercise 4.3: Identify the Levels of Writing Development (pp. 83–85)

Example 1: Scribble

Example 2: Mock letters

Example 3: Random letter string

Example 4: Semiphonetic

Example 5: Phonetic

Example 6: Transitional

Exercise 4.4: Write at Different Levels of Print (p. 88)

Sentence to rewrite: *I want to see an elephant.*

Print Level	Sentence Form
Phonetic	I wont tu ce an lafnt
Semiphonetic	I W T C A L
Random letter string	XXXOOZZZAA
Mock letters	*(handwritten mock letters)*
Scribble	*(scribble)*

Exercise 4.5: Modeling Writing (p. 89)

- What level(s) of print should you model for a child who is:
  — Scribbling?
    - Conventional
    - Random letter strings (with letters in the child's name)
    - Mock letters
  — Using mock letters?
    - Conventional
    - Semiphonetic
    - Random letter strings (with letters in the child's name)
  — Using random letters?
    - Conventional
    - Semiphonetic
    - Phonetic

(continued)

— Writing in a semiphonetic manner?
- **Conventional**
- **Phonetic**
- **Correct sight words**

Reflection and Review (p. 89)

1. Describe the three components of print knowledge.
   - *Print awareness* **(concepts of print)**
   - *Alphabet knowledge* **(letter names and sounds)**
   - *Being a writer* **(writing for a purpose)**

2. What skills do children need to learn in order to understand the alphabetic principle?
   - **Children need to understand the concept of speech sounds (i.e., phonemic awareness) and that letters of the alphabet represent sounds.**

3. Describe the five stages and characteristics of writing development.
   - *Prealphabetic,* **or** *preconventional,* **stage: scribbles, mock letters, random letter strings**
   - *Semiphonetic* **stage: simple sound-letter representations**
   - *Phonetic* **stage: close letter-sound correspondence**
   - *Transitional* **stage: well-developed understanding of the alphabetic principle with orthographic spelling errors**
   - *Conventional* **stage: orthographically and grammatically correct writing**

4. What are developmentally appropriate ways to facilitate the development of print knowledge in young children?
   - *Print awareness*:
     - **Provide multiple exposures to and direct instruction of print, logos, signs, and words.**
     - **Explicitly model how print works.**
   - *Alphabet knowledge*:
     - **Provide multiple exposures to and intentional instruction of letter names and sounds.**
   - *Being a writer*:
     - **Provide lots of opportunities for children to write and to see modeled writing at developmental levels.**

Chapter 5
Assessment Connections

Exercise 5.1: What Assessments Do You Use? (p. 92)
(Answers will vary.)

Exercise 5.2: Categorize Your Assessments (p. 102)
(Answers will vary, depending on responses in *Exercise 5.1*.)
Participants may not have sufficient information to classify their assessments; in that case, they should consult other sources, such as the technical manual of the instrument or information from the publisher.

Exercise 5.3: Identify the Type of Assessment (p. 103)

1. At the beginning of the school year, 15 children in your 4-year-old group looked at a series of picture sets to identify the words that rhyme. According to the authors of the assessment, children at this age are on track to successful early reading if they correctly identify 60 percent or more of the rhyming pairs. Five of your children correctly identified all of the rhyming word pairs, and ten did not, scoring "below benchmark" (i.e., below the level that predicts later success).

   - What type of assessment is this? **This is a screening test.**
   - What do the results tell you? **A few children have learned to rhyme.**
   - What do the results *not* tell you? **The majority has not learned to rhyme.**
   - What should you do after getting this information? **You need to plan rhyming activities to teach them about rhyming and word play.**

2. After conducting rhyming activities for several weeks, you administer the same assessment, having the ten "below benchmark" children look at the picture sets to assess their rhyme-matching skills. This time, five of those children were consistently able to match the word pairs that rhyme.

   - What type of assessment is? **This is a progress-monitoring assessment.**
   - What do the results tell you, and what do you need to do? **More children are learning about rhyme, and a few still need more focused instruction and practice. You need to provide more focused instruction with small groups for the children who are not getting it and continue more general rhyming activities with the other children.**

(continued)

3. Of the five children who were not learning to rhyme, three are making some gains in their rhyming ability; however, two do not seem to be making any gains. These two children also have underdeveloped skills in several other areas.

- What should you do? **Continue with small-group instruction, increase the instruction time, and seek additional assistance from the team, possibly a speech-language pathologist to conduct further diagnostic assessment to identify a possible language delay or disorder.**

Exercise 5.4: Match the Oral Skill to the Language Structure (p. 106)

phonology	Uses speech that is understandable with only age-appropriate errors
semantics	Understands concepts such as *top/bottom, under/over, beginning/middle/end, first/last/next, before/after, one/all, more/less, same/not same*
morphology	Uses word endings that indicate plurals, possessives, present tense, past tense (e.g., **-s, -ing, -ed**)
syntax	Uses sentences with correct word order, of appropriate length, and includes pronouns, verbs, and question forms
prosody	Relates a story with three to five events

Exercise 5.5: Indicate the Progression of Phonological Skills (p. 107)

Phonological Awareness Items	Age Expectation
Rhyme	
<u>Imitates rhythmic patterns in songs, rhymes, and fingerplays</u>	2–3 years
Fills in missing words to known songs, rhymes, and fingerplays	2–3 years
Identifies words that rhyme	3–5 years
Produces a word that rhymes with a given word	4–5 years
Produces a string of three words that rhyme	5–6 years
Blending	
Blends words into syllables (e.g., **cow-boy**)	3–4 years
Blends the beginning sound to the rest of a word (e.g., **f-ish**)	4–5 years
Blends words with three sounds (e.g., **s-u-n**)	4–5 years
Segmenting	
Segments words into syllables	3–4 years
Identifies the number of syllables in words	4–5 years
Identifies words that begin with the same sound	3–5 years
Segments the beginning sound from the rest of a word (e.g., **s-un**)	4–5 years
Segments sounds in words with three sounds (e.g., **h-a-t**)	5–6 years

Exercise 5.6: Match Checklist Items to Your Assessments (p. 108)
(Answers will vary, depending on the assessments that participants are using.)

Answer Key

Reflection and Review (p. 108)

1. List the purposes and uses of assessment.
   - **To identify what children know and what they need to learn.**
   - **To identify children who are not developing at the expected rate.**
   - **To guide programming and instruction.**
   - **To document children's learning and thereby evaluate program effectiveness.**
   - **To communicate with others about your program.**
   - **To identify professional development needs.**

2. What are predictive behaviors that foretell reading development?
   - **Oral language development in sentence structure, vocabulary, and speech intelligibility.**
   - **The ability to play with and manipulate the sound structures of words (i.e., phonological awareness).**
   - **Word retrieval and naming items, objects, and people.**

3. Describe the characteristics of both *norm-referenced* and *criterion-referenced* assessments.
   - *Norm-referenced* **assessments compare a child's performance to a normative sample, or a group of children of the same age or grade level.**
   - *Criterion-referenced* **assessments compare a child's performance to a benchmark or functional level.**

4. Describe both *informal* and *standardized* assessments.
   - *Informal* **assessments consist of results of information about children's skills using observations, checklists, rating scales, and work samples.**
   - *Standardized* **assessments are designed to efficiently sample a child's skills under controlled conditions and are administered in the same way each time.**

5. Describe the components of your assessment procedure that identify children's early literacy skills. **(Answers will vary.)**